D1116662

HOOF PRINTS
More Stories from Proud Spirit

Melanie Sue Bowles

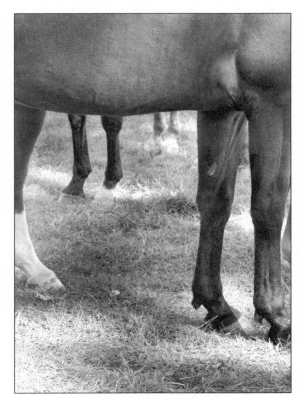

Pineapple Press, Inc.
Sarasota, Florida

Text © 2008 by Melanie Sue Bowles
Photos © 2008 by Melanie Sue Bowles, except page i courtesy of Karen L. Hammett, page 96 courtesy of Cheri Prill, and page 102 courtesy of T.J. Broom.

Inquiries should be addressed to:

Pineapple Press, Inc.
P.O. Box 3889
Sarasota, Florida 34230

www.pineapplepress.com

Library of Congress Cataloging-in-Publication Data
Bowles, Melanie Sue, 1957-
  Hoof prints : more stories from Proud Spirit / Melanie Sue Bowles. -- 1st ed.
    p. cm.
  ISBN 978-1-56164-412-4 (hardback : alk. paper)
  1. Horses--Arkansas--Mena. 2. Horses--Florida--Myakka City. 3. Proud Spirit Horse
Sanctuary (Mena, Ark.) 4. Animal rescue--Arkansas--Mena. 5. Animal rescue--Florida--Myakka
City. 6. Bowles, Melanie Sue, 1957- 7. Horsemen and horsewomen--Arkansas--Mena--
Anecdotes. I. Title.
  SF301.B647 2008
  636.1'0832--dc22

                               2007042814

First Edition
10 9 8 7 6 5 4 3 2 1

Design by Shé Heaton
Printed in the United States of America

*"All of us are watchers—of television, of time clocks,
of traffic on the freeway—but few are observers.
Everyone is looking, not many are seeing."*
—Letters from Side Lake *by Peter M. Leschak*

*This book is dedicated to the memory
of my parents, Rex and Ginny Foster,
who taught me the difference between
just looking and truly seeing.*

Acknowledgments

Jim getting a kiss from Riley

Whenever I write acknowledgments, Jim teasingly asks why he's always mentioned last. So I'm putting him first. Proud Spirit Horse Sanctuary simply would not exist without him. I get calls from all across the country from people seeking my advice on starting up a rescue organization. The first thing I ask them is if their spouse or partner is on board. If they hesitate at all, my response is, "Don't do it." Truthfully, you can't do it. We recently took in all the unadoptable horses from an organization in another state that was shutting down for this very reason. The operator's husband had had enough of the unrelenting work and financial burden and insisted on folding. We hear about this happening all too often and ultimately it's the horses that suffer.

If I had to convince Jim to accept another horse into our program, or stress about handing him another monumental vet, farrier, dental, hay, or feed bill, Proud Spirit would not have remained in operation for as long as it has, nor would it be the tremendous success that it is. I am so deeply grateful for the partnership he and I share. Thank you, Jim, for understanding that it's about giving back to the world around us, but most of all, thank you for understanding that it's about these downtrodden horses who find their way us. I am continually in awe of your selflessness. You are my hero.

When we relocated to Arkansas the new facility needed considerable updating and repair. I would like to thank Charley Grosse for the immaculate fence lines. Your professionalism is exemplary. Thank you to Bob Hostetler and Monte Hostetler for creating sixteen beautiful horse stalls where an old cattle manger used to be. An enormous amount of gratitude goes to Aaron Davis for always being just a phone call away and helping me take care of too many things to list.

Thank you to Chris and Charlena Jenkins for showing up every time we've needed you and for caring about these horses as much as we do. But most of all, thank you for your very dear friendship. Other friends I am in debt to include Ira Nelson for helping us save Indigo's life, and Jean McCormick and Susan Shuman for saving precious little Ruby. Jean gets an additional *huge* thank you for the gentle prodding to finish this book and the hours and hours of proofreading. I am eternally grateful to Gayle Hunt for insisting that I write the first book, *The Horses of Proud Spirit,* and to Colleen Hamilton for her eloquent creation of the PBS special about our rescue work.

I am grateful for my family. I thank my siblings—Maureen, Manitta, Mark, Melinda, and Mathew—for that extraordinary weekend in September of 2007. I'll never forget it and I love you all. An extra special hug to my brother Mark for inspiring in me a love of books and reading, and for caring so deeply about my writing. To my cousin, Susan Haley, thank you for sharing your heart with me and for also caring about my writing as though it were your own. To my nephew, Joshua Foster, for loving this property, our horses, and for tossing three hundred bales of hay while you were here on vacation. And as always, to my niece, Sarah, thank you for sharing your love of horses with me. In my heart you are also my friend and my daughter. To Sarah's husband, Stephen Ross, thank you for embracing this country lifestyle and for allowing Sarah to be who she is.

I am very appreciative of everyone who has helped and continues to help keep our horses healthy: Dr. Mark Davis, DVM (we miss you!); Dr. Donna Craig, DVM; Dr. Leon Mitchell, DVM; and Dr. Randy Burgess, DVM; Certified Equine Dentists Dale Craig and Ben Matheson; Farriers Melissa Ward, Tommy Lehmann, Diana Scott, and Travis Ross.

Lisa Ross-Williams and Kenny Williams are a wealth of information for horse owners everywhere (www.naturalhorsetalk.com). But what makes this information so valuable is their willingness to share. You both have made the lives of countless horses better. Thank you for your generosity and your friendship.

Thank you to Helena Berg, editor extraordinaire. You made the process painless and I am enormously appreciative of your hard work and intelligent input. To Shé Heaton, thank you for all your creativity and hard work in putting the book together. And finally, last but not least, I am tremendously grateful to David and June Cussen. Thank you for believing that the stories about our horses should be told. You've helped change lives.

Contents

The View from the Tailgate

WHENEVER YOU HANDLE HAY, no matter how neat or tightly bound the bales are, little bits and pieces of straw seem to get everywhere. My husband Jim and I had just stacked fifteen heavy bales into the bed of his pickup and were getting ready to take them out to our horses. A gentle breeze was blowing the loose hay around, and somehow it all ended up in my direction. Jim managed to remain completely free of the itchy particles, but it was in my hair, down my britches, inside my shirt, under my collar, and stuck to my sweatshirt. Jim tossed the last bale into the bed of the pickup and jumped into the driver's seat. I looked down at my clothes and thought it best if I—and all the clinging hay—stayed out of the cab. After all, the seats of his truck are upholstered.

We are a two-truck family. We use both of them around our ranch, but Jim and I have different opinions about the definition of a farm vehicle. He likes to keep them clean and looking as new as possible. Especially his. And he manages to do that . . . with his. My truck on the other hand . . . well, that's a different story.

1

The ranch in Florida

So rather than getting in the cab and risking getting hay on his seats, I walked around to the back of the truck and hopped up on the lowered tailgate. I lifted my gloved hand in a wave, high enough for Jim to see in the rearview mirror that I was safely seated for the ride out to where the horses were grazing.

He put the truck in gear and headed down the driveway. I tucked my hands under my legs and lifted my shoulders up high as I breathed in the sweet smell of the hay that was stacked all around me. I smiled and looked out over the pastures at the horses.

A few of them lifted their heads. They knew the routine and stood waiting for us to drive through one of the gates to begin throwing hay off the back of the truck. We usually went to a different place each night to avoid one area of the property being overused and worn down by the horses. They had gotten in the habit of waiting to see which gate we drove though before coming to us. Tonight we were going to the west side of our fifty acres. A creek ran diagonally through our land. When the water was low we could cross it in the truck without a problem, but right now the water was too high, even for the four-wheel drive. To get to the other side we had to go out our front gate, drive a quarter-mile down the county road, and then come in through our neighbor's driveway. There was a gate in our shared fence line that allowed easy access to each other's ranches.

I was enjoying my perspective of the horses and our property from my seat on the tailgate. It was interesting to watch everything slowly recede. When you're facing forward the landscape seems to flash by as you look out the window. But sitting backwards, you have more time to contemplate the scenery. For some reason, this quote ran through my mind: "It's not where you've been that matters, but rather where you're going." I wasn't sure who originally said it, and I wasn't even really sure I had remembered it correctly, but I decided that I didn't agree with it—where you've been matters very much.

I swung my dangling feet back and forth and watched as the dust swirled around my cowboy boots. A sense of peace washed over me. Jim was driving slowly—we used this opportunity every evening to check our fence lines—but I found myself wishing that it would take him a little longer to arrive at the neighbor's gate.

Right at that moment I felt as though I could traverse the entire United States sitting this way. But I would want to stay along the small country roads as in William Least Heat-Moon's *Blue Highways*. And I would want my feet dangling off the back of a pickup truck, just the way they were then, as I watched farms and small towns slowly fade from view like the gentle serenity of dew disappearing before the sun.

When we reached the end of our driveway Jim turned right onto the county road. It was evening and the sun was just lowering in the sky. It hadn't yet reached the horizon, but it was already turning into a huge red ball. I always thought that sunsets in Florida were nearly incomparable. There was a large stand of slash pines at the far end of our pasture. The waning light made the bark on the west side of each tree glow as if they were on fire. I marveled at the way their green boughs turned the same fiery red.

As we drove along the road, I instinctively turned my head to watch the thirty-plus horses who lived with us at Proud Spirit, the sanctuary Jim and I created back in the early '90s for abused, neglected, and unwanted horses. My thoughts went back to the beginning and the horse who started it all. I easily spotted her now out in the herd. She was a tall bay Thoroughbred mare whom I had named Cody. Her lovely forelock reached all the way down to her eyes and the tips had turned golden from the sun. I watched as she ambled along, grazing by herself slightly away from the main herd. She was elderly now and no longer the alpha mare. I recalled a time when no other horse would cross her. But now she walked away when one of them challenged her. She preferred to keep her distance from the rowdiness of the younger ones.

I peered at her more closely. She suddenly looked so old to me. I was, of course, aware of the passing of time. But when did this happen? The muscles along her back were no longer toned and her spine was beginning to show. There was gray around her muzzle and she had developed the deep hollows above her eyes that older horses get. I had noticed lately that she was standing with her head hanging low more often than I saw her grazing, and she was losing weight.

I squeezed my eyes shut for just a second as I shook my head to displace the image. The inevitable loomed in my mind and I couldn't stand the thought of her not being a part of my life. A sad smile crossed my face as I looked back in her direction and recalled the astonishing journey she and I had taken together.

Cody was my first horse. I brought her home back in the early '90s. Jim and I were earning our living as firefighters. We worked twenty-four-hour shifts and routinely saw drownings, heart attacks, vehicle accidents, house fires, and suicides. The job was stressful and exhausting. At that time we lived in town, near our jobs. In an attempt to simplify our lives, we decided to move away from the heavy congestion of the city and buy a small place on five acres out in the country. At least our time away from work would be peaceful.

Our new home was located in an equestrian community and we were surrounded by horses. I had never spent much time around horses. I was never horse-crazy as a kid, and really had no desire to ride as an adult. But for some reason—a reason which was undetermined at the time—I decided that I had to have one. It was a fateful decision that would change our lives and ultimately the lives of numerous horses in need who would find their way to our sanctuary.

Cody was a middle-aged Thoroughbred mare who had been neglected, malnourished, and mistreated. The day I entered her life, she had reached a pinnacle and was fed up with the entire human race. But I was a novice, and all I saw when I looked at her was a tall bay mare with beautiful eyes who needed to be brushed and maybe gain a few pounds. I thought she was perfect and ignorantly paid much more for her than someone with any amount of horse knowledge would have paid. As her health improved under my care, dangerous problems and a difficult personality emerged, which I was ill-equipped to handle. Unfortunately, because of my inexperience, I didn't realize that her dull coat and bad feet were the result of years of neglect. She had also been handled roughly her entire life, which was the reason she viewed humans as the enemy. When I got on her back she was ready to explode. Others advised that Cody could not have been a worse choice for me. I was told over and over to sell her.

But I determined that this mare was not at fault—the humans in her life were the ones who had failed. And her mistreatment would end with me. After months of being unable to ride her, struggling to handle her on the ground, and receiving lots of unsavory advice, I finally realized that I needed to educate *myself* about communicating with horses. I made a commitment to Cody and she helped me understand that this is a partnership.

She showed me how to help her trust again and she is the reason I am dedicated to never stop learning their language. She changed my life and essentially the life of every hurting equine who ever found its way to us in the subsequent years to come.

At the start of this journey, I barely knew how to put a halter on a horse. As my experience and knowledge evolved I was able to confidently and safely work with "difficult" horses that others had given up on, ultimately giving them back their lives.

In the beginning I was in awe of an entire list of nationally known trainers, clinicians, and gurus. Over the years I have even met several of them in person. They are all good horsemen and -women; some impressed me more than others, however, as a few are clearly driven by their egos. Regardless, they all are imparting valuable natural training techniques from their instruction, without a doubt, and all of them are good at what they do. But I eventually realized that what they were really great at was marketing their training DVDs, along with the specialized equipment stamped with their names and logos. There's certainly nothing wrong with this, in my opinion. They deserve their success; hundreds of people, and horses, have benefited from their programs and have better relationships. The limit, for me, was when I came to understand that these clinicians do not deserve star-quality reverence from their fans. Since beginning my dedication to horses, over 150 have come through Proud Spirit. They have been the genuine teachers.

Cody was the reason that Proud Spirit Horse Sanctuary existed and the genesis of my lifelong commitment to taking in horses that no one else wanted. For the journey of lessons and learning that she took me on, knowing what I know now, I would pay ten times what I paid for her back then. Even more. To me, she was priceless. She deserved our awe for what she had survived before she came to Proud Spirit, and for the way she eventually learned to trust again and how she fully gave me her heart. All the horses who endure abuse and neglect, but continue to trust, are the ones who deserve our reverence.

• • •

Jim turned into our neighbor's driveway and pulled up to the gate in our shared fence line. I slid off the back of the truck and went to unlatch the chain. I scrambled back up into the bed, and as we drove out to our own pasture I took out my pocket knife and started cutting the twine off each bale. The horses had been keeping their eyes on us. Most of them had stopped grazing and had lifted their heads, waiting and watching for the hay to start hitting the ground. Jim steered the truck in a widening circle while I tossed flakes of hay over the side of the bed. Suddenly, as though they were one, the entire herd began moving in our direction, first at a walk and then they came galloping across the field and crashing through the creek. It was a ritual they were used to, and it was also my favorite time of the day.

I stopped tossing the hay for just a moment to watch them running. It was a breathtaking sight, and even after living with thirty-plus horses for over twelve years, it still gave me chills. Their flashing hooves and dancing manes reflected the pride in my heart over the life Jim and I were able to give these horses— a life free from being locked in stalls and small dirt paddocks. They are allowed the freedom of movement which horses desperately need to thrive. They have natural manes and tails, whiskers on their muzzles, and hair in their ears, and their hooves are given natural trims and left bare without the restriction of detrimental shoes. But most importantly, they function as a herd, safe in the companionship of other horses.

Once the hay had been distributed and the entire herd was munching their dinner, Jim pulled his truck over to the side and shut the engine down. He got out of the cab and took a spot on the dropped tailgate while I went out to walk among the horses. I liked to check them several times a day to make sure no one had any cuts or wounds, and to simply give everyone a gentle rub and say hello. I navigated among the herd and everyone was doing fine.

I lingered with Cody for several minutes. She stopped mid-chew and lifted her head up to rest against my chest. I pulled her to me and spoke quietly, "How's my beautiful girl?"

She resumed grinding the hay in her mouth but didn't move away. I leaned down and kissed her eye, and then I made a circle around her and gently brushed her coat with my bare hand. I returned to her head and she had once more buried her nose in the hay. I leaned down and cupped my hand over her eye. She didn't stop eating as she let me close her soft lid.

Finally, I began walking back to Jim. He saw me heading in his direction and slid off the tailgate to go start the truck.

"Hang on a second," I called out. "Can we sit out here for a minute?"

"Sure," he said, and repositioned himself on the tailgate. I jumped up beside him.

"What's up?" he asked.

"Nothin'," I said. "I just wanted to sit for a minute. Watch the horses."

Jim nodded and looked out in the direction of the pasture. The horses were standing in the same circular pattern of the hay that we had just put out for them. I looked down at my feet swinging back and forth.

"Well," I said after a moment, "there is something I think we need to talk about." I was still contemplating my boots. I smartly tapped my toes together a few times before I glanced up at him. He remained quiet and continued watching the horses. "Do you ever think about all this?" I asked, squinting up at him.

"Think about all what?"

"The horses . . . the responsibility of this many horses. The amount of money we spend. The time and energy we devote to all this. Do you ever think about it all?"

Jim lifted his shoulders just slightly and tipped his head to the side. He screwed up his mouth just a little and narrowed his eyes. "Not really," he said and let his shoulders fall back into place.

He was definitely a man of few words. We rarely had deep or

lengthy conversations. I was used to it. For Jim, things simply are what they are. And he isn't one to ponder a situation or fret about the way something is going to work out. Fretting and pondering is my department.

It was winter of 2004. We had been earning our living as fire-fighters since the '80s and we were nearing retirement now. Jim and I would both still be in our forties. I knew that he and I wanted the same things when we were finally able to leave the fire department. We had always talked about moving out of Florida. It was getting too crowded and too expensive, and we were tired of the heat. We wanted four distinct seasons. I longed for autumn and we both dreamed about living in the mountains.

We needed no discussion about *where* we would spend our retirement, but we needed to talk about *how*. I knew, without a shadow of a doubt, how I wanted to spend the rest of my life—running this horse sanctuary. But Proud Spirit began as my dream. Even though Jim was just as committed as I was to these horses that no one else wanted, did he want to spend the next half of his life tied to this unyielding responsibility?

"So, what are you getting at?" he asked. He picked up a piece of straw from the bed of the truck and twirled it between his thumb and forefinger.

"Well," I began as I looked out over the horses. And as though he needed a visual aid, I waved my hand in their direction and continued, "We've been taking care of almost forty hors-es on a daily basis for over twelve years." He nodded in confir-mation, but remained quiet. "We've made a lot of sacrifices," I said. "This has been a lot of work. If we ever manage to go on vacation, we can't even go at the same time. We never go out to dinner. And you," I paused for just a second and stopped swing-ing my feet back and forth, "you gave up your Harley," I said qui-etly and looked up at him.

For years, Jim had dreamed of owning a Harley-Davidson motorcycle. After a few promotions and a couple pay raises at the fire department, he finally bought the bike of his dreams: a black-

and-white Heritage Special. A short time later we were given an opportunity to purchase the fifty acres we now owned. It was our chance to expand the sanctuary and continue our rescue work. But the only way we could make it happen was if he let his bike, and the monthly payment, go. I cried for him the day he sold it, but he consoled me by saying, "It's only a chunk of metal. These horses are more important." That was back in 1996.

Today Jim looked down at the piece of straw he was holding and then stuck it in his mouth. He pursed his lips around it and nodded thoughtfully when I reminded him of that sacrifice he made. He cocked an eyebrow and looked down at me sitting beside him. "What are you getting at?" he asked again.

I smacked him on the arm with the back of my hand. "You dope." I laughed. "You know what I'm getting at. We're about to retire. I think we need to make absolutely sure that we are on the same page about these horses. Should we just make a final commitment to the ones we have and stop taking in any more? Eventually we'd be down to only a few horses. We would have the freedom to do some things, travel or whatever. Or are we going to make this sanctuary, and possibly even more horses, something we are committed to for the rest of our lives?"

Jim nodded slowly as he rolled the piece of straw from the left side of his mouth to the right, but again he remained quiet.

"When we retire and sell this place," I went on, "the decision we make about the sanctuary is going to affect everything we do from here on out. It'll determine what kind of property we buy, how much land . . . everything."

Jim nodded once again and returned the piece of straw to the left side of his mouth. I resumed swinging my feet back and forth. We both looked over at the horses.

"Well," I finally said.

"Well, what?" he answered.

I smacked him on the arm again. He quickly snatched my hand in his before I could pull it back. "What do you think I'm going to say?" He laughed while he tugged on my arm. "This is our life. These horses are our life. I wouldn't change a thing."

"Are you sure?" I said with my eyes filling up with tears.

He released my hand and put his arms around me. We leaned against each other and I waited for his answer. "I'm sure," he said quietly. "I've never been more sure of anything in my life." I turned my face into his chest and started sobbing joyful tears.

"Why are you crying?"

I didn't answer him, but thought to myself, geez, men are so stupid. I also thought that I could not love him any more than I did right then. And so I wept harder. My face remained smashed against him as I sniffled and snorted. After a few moments he withdrew his arms from around me, gripped both my shoulders in his big hands, and gently moved me away from him. He looked down unhappily at the mess my leaking eyes and dripping nose had made on his sweatshirt.

"Sorry," I said with a shrug as I wiped my nose with the sleeve of my own sweatshirt.

He just nodded as we stared at each other in silence. And then we both began to smile. I kept my eyes on his and put my head down demurely as I envisioned a romantic moment between us.

"Can we get back to the house now?" he asked. And then he stole a quick glance at his watch. "*StarGate SG-1* starts in fifteen minutes."

Jiggy and the Junk Shops

THE TELEPHONE CONVERSATION STARTED OUT just a little odd. "Name's Jiggy," said the voice on the other end when I answered the phone. There was no greeting in response to my "hello" when I picked up, no inquiry about who was speaking or whether or not he had reached Proud Spirit. Just the firm pronouncement of, "Name's Jiggy."

"Jiggy?" I repeated.

"Mmm-hmm," the man said. "Tha's right."

"Okay," I smiled. "What can I do for ya, Jiggy?"

"They's a horse here, he cain't work no more. Boss sez I'm to take 'im on back and shoot 'im." I winced anytime someone said this to me. Some people feel this is a quick and painless way to end the life of a horse. But unless there is an emergency that requires immediate action, it's not something I could ever advocate. For me, for my horses, their passing must be peaceful and humanely administered by a veterinarian. I want my hands gently soothing them to be the last thing they feel and I want my

Max at Proud Spirit

voice to be the last thing they hear, not the ear-shattering report of a bullet to the head.

"I ain't got the heart ta do it," Jiggy continued. "I saw this colt hit the groun' the day he was born 'bout eighteen year ago. He's worked harder than any horse I've ever known. He don't deserve

13

this. I'm wonderin' can you take 'im?"

"Where is the horse? Where're you calling from?"

"I run the stables here at the Triple M Ranch. We got us the finest herd of Aberdeen-Angus cattle in north central Florida and the bes' string of horses for workin' 'em."

"I'm not familiar with the Triple M. Where exactly is it?"

"We set jus' northeast of Mount Dora."

"Mount Dora, huh? That's about three hours from me." Jiggy remained quiet on the other end of the line, seemingly unconcerned about the geographical relationship between our two ranches. "Does the horse belong to you?" I asked.

"No. I care about him like he's my own, but he b'long to the Triple M. They want 'im gone and I ain't got a say."

"They want him shot," I said. Jiggy once again remained quiet. "Well, I have the room to take your horse here. I suppose we could work something—"

"Oh, that's jus' fine!" Jiggy interrupted. "I surely do thank you. Can you come get 'im soon, this weekend?"

"Now, hang on. We just need to talk about a few more things."

Jiggy chuckled. "Ain't nothin' ever simple," he said.

"No, sir, nothin' ever is." I laughed, and shook my head thinking about how my dad used to say the exact same thing. "It's just that if I drive all the way up there I want to make sure whoever owns the Triple M isn't going to give me any grief about taking this horse. I need something in writing saying that they'll turn him over to me."

"Mmm-hmm. All right."

"I need to have a clean Coggins."

"He got that. My stable's run proper."

"And any horse that comes here needs to be able to function in a herd."

"Max get along fine in the herd, he jus' cain't work no more. He gettin' the arthritis." Jiggy paused for just a second then asked, "Anythin' else?"

"No, sir. But I don't have a trailer. I'll have to call you back about when I can come get him. I'll see if a friend can help me out, or I'll borrow one. Unless you can bring him down here?"

"I'd be pleased to do it, but I'd have ta use a ranch trailer and the owner wouldn't go for that. Wastin' time and burnin' rubber on a horse he want shot."

I already figured as much, but made no comment about it. "Okay, Jiggy. We got us a deal. I'll phone you later and let you know when I can come up."

"I don't know your name," he said.

"Mel."

"Mel? You don' sound like no truck driver!"

I started laughing. "Short for Melanie."

"Now, ain't that a pretty name. Why you call yourse'f Mel when you got such a pretty name?"

"My mom would love you, Jiggy," I told him. "She hated anyone shortening my name."

Jiggy and I talked amiably for a few more minutes. I had a hard time picturing what he might look like, but the timbre and cadence of his voice was warm and friendly. I assumed he was Southern born and bred. I also guessed he was probably elderly. Aside from the length of time he told me he'd been at the Triple M, he spoke with the confident wisdom that only comes from living a long time, and he sounded just a little tired. I was looking forward to meeting this gentleman and already felt we were kindred spirits by the way he spoke about the horses. We were just about to hang up when I thought of something else.

"Say, aren't there lots of good junk shops up around there?" I asked. "I love junkin'."

"Well, if you likes junkin', as you call it, this is the place to be," he laughed. It was a rich, hearty laugh that came from deep down in his belly.

I borrowed Sarah's trailer for the trip to bring Max back to Proud Spirit. I also decided to phone my very close friend, Deborah, to see if she wanted to go with me. She's not much on horses, but we have a shared love of ferreting around antique shops. She and I decided to clear our books the following weekend and ditch the husbands, laundry, horses (mine), and kids (hers), and head off to Mount Dora. Neither one of us had ever been there, but we both had heard from various other friends that the town was a junker's dream.

To really do it right, we decided to get up there Friday afternoon. We'd find the Triple M, leave the trailer with Jiggy, and then get a hotel room. That night we would have a relaxing dinner with lots of yakking and catching up. The following day we would rise early to hit the trash and treasure trail before going to pick up the horse Saturday afternoon. It sounded like pure heaven as both Deb and I have very hectic lives that don't leave much room for an escape such as this. Plus it had been quite a while since she and I had been able to spend quality time together.

Jiggy had given me excellent directions to the Triple M. I turned into the entrance of the expansive ranch and drove across the cattle guard. The long dirt road cut through several thousand acres of pasture. We could see numerous out buildings and barns in the distance. I pulled my truck up to the first one we came to—a long row of shed stalls. There appeared to be an office or living quarters adjacent to the barn area. An elderly man came out of the door and stood on the porch that ran across the front of the building. I got out of my truck and walked around the hood. "I'm looking for Jiggy," I said.

"'Course you are," the man said. "Pretty ladies is always lookin' for Jiggy." He made two quick little clucking sounds and winked as he pointed a finger at me like someone pretending to fire a gun. I smiled broadly at his sassiness. I knew by his voice that I had found him, but I asked anyway. "You him?"

He came down off the porch and took a few steps towards me. He extended his hand as he drew closer. "Name's Jiggy," he said as he made a slight bow and elegantly took my hand in his. "Melanie," he added, before I could respond, "I surely thank you." He nodded toward the trailer. I smiled into his dark twinkling eyes.

"I'm glad I could help," I told him

Jiggy was a small man, not much taller than my five foot three inches. In the glow of the fading sunlight his dark black skin took on the color of rich mahogany. He wore a crisp, clean, blue plaid long-sleeved shirt tucked neatly into jeans that appeared brand new. The only thing he was wearing that was worn was the sweat-stained John Deere ball cap on his head. His white hair stuck out from underneath it like a cottony halo.

Deb had come to stand beside us and I introduced her. "Jiggy, this is my friend Deb."

He took her hand just as he had with mine, but he tisked in disdain. "Such pretty girls ruinin' their pretty names." He shook his head sadly and said, "May I call you Deborah? I'm a-guessin' tha's the name your mama gave you." Deb . . . er, *Deborah* smiled at him, as charmed as I was, and told him she would be honored.

"Hey," I said through a smile, "speaking of names—is Jiggy the name your mama gave you?"

He tipped his head back and laughed. "Naw," he said. "Tha's jus' what they call me from my younger days, ya see."

"Yeah, and why's that?" I asked.

"Well, it's like this," he said. He removed his cap then ran a leathery tough hand across his chin. "I had me a reputation with the ladies for, ah, well, gettin' jiggy with it." He made those two little clucking sounds again, winked, and pointed his finger at me. "If ya know what I mean."

"Jiggy with it?" I asked, shaking my head.

He shuffled his feet in a smart little dance and said, "You know—"

I didn't know and looked over at Deb. She shook her head and shrugged. "You mean," I began, and then tried to mimic his moves with my feet, "you were a good dancer."

We stared at each other for just a second. Jiggy regarded me through squinted eyes as I stood there grinning like an idiot.

Finally he spoke. "Mmm-hmm, tha's right," he said, nodding ever so slowly. "I was a good daaancer." He drew the word out in a mocking tone.

Suddenly Deborah and I got it at just about the same time. Deborah inhaled sharply and slapped her hand over her mouth. Her father is an extremely well-mannered, and rather stoic, highly respected physician. On the other hand, I grew up with Rex; this innuendo of Jiggy's was nothing, a cakewalk, compared to some of the things my father said and did. I burst out laughing.

"C'mon," he said, and motioned for us to follow. "Lemme introduce you to Max."

The little gelding was standing in an immaculate box stall and he poked his head over the top of the door as we approached. He was a deep bay color. His black points stood out beautifully from his red coat. This coloring gave his nose the most adorable heart shape and I was immediately smitten.

"Hey there, handsome man," I cooed. Max leaned forward and blew gently through his nostrils. I leaned over to him and blew back. "Wanna come home with me?" I asked.

He popped his lips in response and I smiled at him. The horse was just as sweet as could be. He had the softest eyes hidden behind a curling forelock that was bleached from his years of working in the sun. His movements were gentle and slow. Although he was in wonderful condition for having been ridden so hard for most of his eighteen years—a testament to the care he had received from Jiggy—he clearly could no longer do ranch work. His retirement to Proud Spirit was certainly deserved. I would be pleased to make him a part of our family.

Jiggy helped me unhook the horse trailer. I gave him a ballpark time that Deborah and I would return the following afternoon. We said good-bye to him and Max and left the Triple M. We arrived back on the outskirts of town about an hour later. It was easy to find accommodations along the main drag. After we had our hotel key in hand, we headed into the shopping district just as it started to pour down rain. It was nearing seven o'clock now and a lot of the shops were closed. Undaunted by the rain and the time, we drove around the quaint little town, plotting our course for the next day of treasure hunting. Deb spotted a local restaurant and we had a wonderfully relaxing dinner with even better conversation.

The following morning I awoke at my usual time, around five-thirty. I was too excited to go back to sleep, but knowing that Deb is not a morning person I somehow managed to stay quiet for another hour and a half. She and I had been close friends since our early twenties. I knew how long it would take her to get ready. And so, just a little after seven, I began pestering her to start the day. I whipped open the hotel curtains, allowing the morning sun to illuminate the room while I cheerfully cajoled her to get out of bed. Deb groaned from underneath her pillow, called me a few unsavory names, and finally staggered to the shower.

She and I are definitely a study in contrasts. I have no children and cringe with irritation when I hear a kid cry. My horses are my babies, my hands are rough, my nails are chipped and broken, and I haven't a clue about fashion. My morning ritual consists of showering, drying off, and running a comb through my hair—that's it. I usually wear comfy jeans and baggy T-shirts and do not even own one tube of mascara or eye shadow or blush.

Conversely, Deborah is the mother of four. She is one of the most nurturing and maternal women I know. When she hears a child cry, even if it's not her own, she looks soulfully toward the sound, places a hand over her heart, and moans, "Aww." She always looks perfectly coifed; her immaculate toenails are painted the same color as her perfectly manicured fingernails, her outfits are flattering and feminine, and I could fit a saddle in her make-up bag. Doing her hair involves an elaborate ritual of several different-sized brushes used in conjunction with the blow dryer while an array of curling irons heats up on the side. And then everything is held in place with smelly sprays and gels. And apparently there is a clear and definite need for the two separate applications: one is for "holding" and one is for "scrunching."

Frankly, it all mystifies me and I can do nothing but shake my befuddled head when witnessing this ritual.

But however odd it may seem, we cherish each other's differences, love each other dearly for who we are, and most importantly, we both have a hearty passion for junkin'.

We found the perfect parking place shortly after ten o'clock and headed down the first street of stores with excited anticipation. The first door we came to was a gourmet coffee shop. We peeked in the window, glanced at each other, and both shook our heads in silent agreement not to bother going in. We were searching for junk. Antiques. Used stuff. We wanted to sift through tons of trash until we found treasure!

We walked briskly to the next shop. The sign out front held more promise. It read "Carol's Curiosities." Upon entering we were overwhelmed by shelf after shelf of revoltingly cute glass kittens, ducks, and puppies in various shades of pastel pink and blue. And, well, finding nothing very curious about any of this, we both did an about-face and exited Carol's.

Not in the least bit discouraged, we forged ahead to the next shop. As we looked in the window we saw T-shirts, wind socks, cutting boards, and paperweights, all proudly emblazoned with the town's name to take home as a souvenir. "Hmm," we simultaneously intoned. Deb peered further along the street and noticed a sign for fudge three doors down. We glanced at each other and solemnly nodded. While we were en route to the fortification only chocolate can provide at a time like this, we passed a real estate office and a candle shop.

Together Deb and I inhaled deeply as we entered the fudge shop. We were attempting to displace the overpowering scent of every conceivable spice and flower known to man that oozed from the candle shop next door. Not necessarily a bad thing, but we wanted to smell dust and find things covered in dirt, screaming with character from the chipped paint and dents of old age.

"I'll just have a tiny taste of the maple," I said to the young lady behind the counter.

"How's this?" she asked as she placed her spatula along the slab of fudge.

"A little bigger," I said. I motioned with my hand for her to move the spatula like I was helping to back a large truck into a tight parking space.

"That's good," I finally said, satisfied with the bigger portion. I heard Deb snickering behind me, saying something in a questioning tone of voice about "you call that small and tiny?" The bored teenager cut my piece of maple fudge, wrapped it in waxed paper, and then turned her attention to Deb.

"I'll have the turtle tracks," she said. "'Cept make it a little smaller than hers."

"Sissy," I muttered under my breath as I bit into my modest chunk.

Back out on the street we dejectedly strolled along while not one single shop window compelled us to put away our fudge and step inside to see their wares. We came upon a gourmet bakery shop for dogs. Just so the shopping trip wasn't a total loss, I decided to go in and get my pups a special treat to take back home. As I paid the clerk behind the counter of the "barkery," I lamented our dismay at finding nothing but a town gone tourism. The teenage boy nodded unsympathetically as he took my money and handed me my bag of liver cookies.

I joined Deb, who was waiting on the sidewalk. I suddenly had a thought. "Can I use your cell phone?" I asked. She rummaged around in her bag and handed it to me without questioning who I was calling. I stepped into a small alley to get away from the noise of the street. Jiggy answered on the second ring.

"Jiggy!" I cried. "I need your help."

"Well, what's wrong, lil' miss?"

"I'm standing here on Main Street and I'm not lookin' at any junk. All I'm lookin' at is a bunch of tourists buying dopey pink glass kittens and wind socks covered with cows wearing stupid hair bows."

Jiggy burst out laughing. "You in the wrong part a' town!

Jiggy'll set ya right," he crowed through his mirth.

Armed with the directions Jiggy had given me, I made my way through the crowd back to where Deborah waited. "C'mon!" I commanded, as I grabbed her arm and started propelling her toward my truck.

"What? Where are we going?" she asked as I pushed her through the crowd.

"I've found our junk!" I told her. "Let's get to the truck."

We followed the directions that Jiggy had given me and left the main drag. We had gone about a mile when we came to a curve in the road. Suddenly, there before us, we saw a row of old buildings with nothing but delicious trash spilling out of their doors. There was an open-air flea market teeming with vendors across the street, and next to that, a football-field-size industrial brown building with *Antique Mall* painted in huge red letters across its rusty metal roof. It was all within sight of where I had just slammed on the brakes and all we could do was stare gap-mouthed in awe. Suddenly Deborah nudged my shoulder and brought me out of my trance.

"Park!" was all she said.

We hardly knew where to begin but ended up in the dirt parking lot across from the flea market. We decided to walk the short distance to the antique mall, then cross the street to the junky shops. We would have made better time had Deborah not insisted on wearing open-toed, high-heeled sandals, although she would have doggedly pointed out that they perfectly completed her ensemble.

The rest of the day played out just as we had dreamed it would. Deborah found several items to complete the transformation that was taking place in her newly redecorated kitchen. I hadn't purchased anything yet but really didn't care; I was having the time of my life as I spirited through the piles and stacks and rows of trash. We were contentedly walking down the main aisle of the antique mall, stopping here and there to examine something that caught our eye. All of a sudden I spotted "it" about twenty feet away. I stopped dead in my tracks and clutched Deborah's arm.

Up high on a shelf, back behind a collection of wooden duck decoys and porcelain doorknobs, I could just make out his colorful comb. I hadn't said a word, but Deborah understood immediately the significance of what I must have found by my reaction. She knew my current mission was roosters. She turned her head in the direction of my glassy-eyed gaze and searched the shelves. "Where?" she quietly whispered.

"There," I whispered back, discreetly pointing to the rooster. I didn't want to alert other junkers who were standing closer to the treasure I had just spotted and might possibly get to him before me.

Deb lifted a few of the duck decoys out of the way as I carefully reached up and clasped my hands around one of the most beautiful china roosters I had ever seen. He was perfect. I looked at Deb. She smiled, just as happy as I was over this find, and said, "He's perfect, Mel."

He was exactly what I didn't even dare hope to find. I had been collecting these roosters for quite a while. I only had four of them, but this one I now held in my hands was far and away the best; he was good sized, in outstanding condition, and his colors were simply glorious. This particular style of rooster was also getting harder and harder to find, and more and more expensive. The last one I had purchased was thirty-five dollars, but he was very small and even had some tiny chips. So before I got too attached to the one I now held in my hands, I had to make sure I could afford him.

I swallowed hard, held my breath, and slowly turned him over. The little sticker on his underside said fifteen dollars. My brow furrowed and I repeated the price to Deb in the form of a question. How could that be? Obviously the proprietor of this booth had no conception of the rooster's worth, for forty to fifty dollars would not have been out of line at all! I looked at the sticker again. It clearly said fifteen dollars.

I certainly have my faults, but I consider myself an extremely honest person. It is, however, absolutely, thoroughly, and genetically impossible for me to buy anything from a junk shop, antique mall, or flea market without dickering. Regardless of how good a deal something is at the price it is marked, I simply must offer less. Period. I would have this rooster and I would have him for less than fifteen dollars or my grandmother's name was not Sadie Reed.

There was an elderly woman manning the little booth. She sat on a hard metal stool and smiled at me from atop her perch as I walked over to her makeshift counter. It was put together out of sawhorses and plywood, and draped in colorful gingham.

"Are ya wantin' that little rooster?" she sweetly asked as she brushed a stray wisp of gray hair off her forehead. "He's a purty feller, ain't he?"

I was completely unfazed by her soft eyes and gentle voice. In one perfectly executed display I shrugged indifferently, sniffed the air, sucked on a tooth, then casually offered her ten bucks. I raised one eyebrow and stared her down. She didn't know what hit her—or so I thought. But then the old gal's eyes hardened and she stared right back. We settled on twelve. I made my obligatory "face of resignation for being taken" and started peeling off bills while gleefully trying to hide my soaring delight.

Several hours later, Deborah and I were back at my truck. We stowed our treasures and then headed out for the Triple M to pick up Max and return home. Jiggy met us out by the barn as I was hooking up my trailer. "Well, now," he called out, "was your day of junkin' a success?" I told him it was and thanked him for saving the day.

"Is Max ready to go?" I asked.

"Mmm-hmm," Jiggy nodded. "I already said my g'bye to the old boy. I reckon I'll miss him a mite." He looked off toward a group of buildings. "Boss'll be right down with that paperwork you wanted. Then you gals can be on your way."

Just as he said the words a dark green pickup truck came

along the dirt road and parked in front of the barn. A tall, heavy-set man got out and walked over to where we stood. "This the gal I tol' you about," Jiggy said to the man. Jiggy set his hand on my shoulder. "Melanie, this here's Boss," he continued.

The tall man stuck out his hand and we shook. "How're ya doin'?" he said. The several times that Jiggy had mentioned "Boss," I thought he was referring to *the* boss, but this was the man's moniker. He immediately turned his attention to Jiggy. "I got bad news, Jig," he said.

"What's that, Boss?"

Boss put his fists on his hips and looked off across the pastures. "Mr. Mason wants four hundred dollars for Max. Cash."

"*What!*" I exclaimed. I shot a look to Jiggy. His expression never changed. But I was furious. "Who's Mr. Mason?" I asked.

"He's the owner of the Triple M," Boss answered.

"You have *got* to be kidding!" I growled. "He wanted him shot!" Jiggy had removed his ball cap and was rubbing his chin.

"You know how he is," Boss said, looking at Jiggy. "Nothin' leaves here unless it brings in a buck." He swung his gaze over to me. "He says he don't know you and you might sell the horse off and make more than four hundred in the deal."

"I can give him references!"

"Won't matter," said Jiggy. "The man want four hun'erd, tha's what you'll give 'im."

"The hell I will," I muttered and folded my arms across my chest. "The lousy—" Jiggy shot me an admonishing glance, quieting me. I was immediately rebuked and smiled conciliatorily, trying to remain in his good graces. I also knew that I'd pay the money.

"I've got a hundred here in my purse, Mel," Deborah said.

I mouthed a "thanks" in her direction. "I'll have to go find a bank for the rest," I told Jiggy and Boss.

"No you won't," Jiggy spoke up and disappeared through the door that was connected to the barn. He came back out shortly and handed Boss a wad of bills. Boss nodded solemnly. "I'm sorry,

Jig," he said, and then reached into his truck and withdrew an envelope off the seat. "Max's papers and vet records," he said as he handed it to me. He clapped Jiggy on the shoulder with a shake of his head and then was gone.

"You didn't have to do that," I said.

"Well, sure I did. You didn't go into this here ta spend your own money." He looked down at the ground and shook his head. "I'm mighty grateful you givin' Max a home." I stood quietly. "B'sides," he continued, "what else I got ta spend my money on? I'm too ol' for romancin' the ladies."

I hooked my thumbs in the belt loops of my jeans and grinned at Jiggy. "Now why don't I believe that?" We both started laughing. Jiggy gave Max one final affectionate pat on the neck. "You b'have yourse'f, ol' man," he said. "I'm gonna miss you." Jiggy's voice wavered just a little. I felt a catch in my own throat and looked away. Finally Jiggy turned and handed me Max's lead rope. The gentle horse loaded without incident. Deborah had already said good-bye to Jiggy and was waiting in the truck.

Jiggy and I walked to the driver's side and shook hands. "Say, you never told us your real name," I said as he released my hand. "The one your mama gave you."

Jiggy put his hands on his hips. "Joe," he said with a nod. "Joseph Isaiah Goodchild."

"Well, Joseph Isaiah Goodchild, my life will never be the same for having met you, sir," I told him. We smiled at each other. I reached for the door handle and gave it a tug as he turned to walk away. But suddenly there was something I needed to know. I left the door ajar and took a few steps in his direction.

"Say, Jiggy!" I called out. He stopped and turned to face me. "I need to ask. Why'd you do this?" I tipped the top of my head back to the trailer where Max quietly stood inside waiting to go to Proud Spirit.

Jiggy removed his ball cap and looked down at the ground. He ran a hand over his clean-shaven chin and then swung his gaze back up to look into my eyes. "Why did you?" he asked.

"Hey, no fair," I laughed. "You can't answer a question with a question." He didn't say anything. He just cocked one eyebrow and smiled ever so slightly.

In an instant I decided that this remarkable man was entitled to an answer. And more than my usual pat answer of, "Oh, I just like horses." I stood quietly as I thought about why I do this—take in all these horses that no one else wants. For just a moment I shifted my eyes away from the older man. I scanned the endless pastures of the vast ranch as if searching for the right words to answer his question. Then my eyes returned to Jiggy. His face was so kind. I felt there was a tremendous amount of understanding between us where no words were said. I wasn't really sure I even needed to answer him.

"I guess—" I began. "I guess it's not very complicated. I believe that every horse should have a dignified and peaceful life, right on up to the end. Otherwise, I suppose I'd say it's a pretty selfish way to go through life, arrogant really, to think an animal no longer deserves our care when we can't get work or ribbons or offspring out of them anymore. I believe they have value beyond what we can get out of them."

I shrugged my shoulders, wondering if he expected me to say more. My eyes remained on Jiggy. He slowly nodded and a small smiled played across his face, reaching all the way into his deep black eyes. Suddenly he made those little clucking sounds, winked, and pointed his "guns" at me. Our eyes locked for just a moment more in total and complete understanding and I swallowed hard. And then I playfully returned his sassy gesture. He tipped his head back and laughed.

On the way out the gates of the Triple M, I said Jiggy's name to myself, "Joseph Isaiah Goodchild—" I said it once again, but out loud this time. Suddenly it hit me.

"Ha!" I yelled.

"What?" Deb asked, looking over at me.

"Joseph Isaiah Goodchild. Those are his initials! J.I.G. Jig, Jiggy."

We both started laughing. "Why, you ol' dog," I muttered. "Gettin' jiggy with it indeed!"

All the way home I couldn't stop smiling as I recalled the remarkable Joseph Isaiah Goodchild. I knew I would never forget him. Ever. And I also knew that every time I looked at Max my heart would fill with memories of Jiggy.

I was also quite pleased with my wonderful find as I pictured this new fifth rooster being placed among the others. Part of my excitement was due to the fact that he was indeed the fifth one. All symbiotics are off for me, in regards to decorating, when there is an even number in one of my collections. I like odd numbers.

I pulled in the driveway at Proud Spirit. Jim met me over by the barn to help unhook the trailer and I introduced him to Max. "Hey, buddy," Jim said and ran his big hand over the gelding's back. "He looks like a nice little guy, huh?"

"He sure is," I answered. I spent about an hour with Max getting him settled in and showing him his new home. He was remarkably calm and behaved as though he'd been here for years. I was so grateful he was with us and that we could provide him this time to just simply be a horse.

I finally made my way up to the house. Jim was kneeling down in the driveway polishing the tires of his truck, a task I never could quite understand. He straightened from his work as I approached. I was eager now to place my new rooster with the others.

"Hey, did you have a good time hittin' the junk shops?" he called out as I breezed by.

"Oh, yeah," I said. I was carrying the rooster, still safely wrapped in newspaper. I lifted him into the air and brandished him high over my head as though I were a prizefighter.

"Well, I'm glad you're home," Jim said. I thought I heard him mumble something about being out of clean underwear.

"I missed you, too," I called over my shoulder as I tried to hide my impatience at being kept from placing the new rooster with the others. But he detained me yet again.

"Hey, Bill and Susan called earlier," he said. "They want to know if we'd like to meet for dinner tonight."

"Um, we'll talk about it in a minute," I hollered from the doorway. I turned and dashed into the kitchen.

I stood at the center island with my treasure and took a deep breath of satisfaction. I carefully removed the newspaper. I let out another big sigh while admiring my terrific find. I couldn't help but smirk as I relived my bargaining finesse. Twelve dollars! It was almost criminal. I innocently turned around to face the fridge and look up at my collection of four roosters. I expected them to be looking back at me cheerfully when I noticed that there were only three!

"What happened?" I said out loud to myself in disbelieving horror. I ran to the back door and out to the driveway.

"What happened to one of my roosters?" I croaked to Jim.

"Oh, that." His tone was casual as he straightened once again from polishing his tires. He paused to admire the gleaming rubber before turning to look in my direction where I stood nearing collapse. "Relax, honey," he continued. "I spilled a Coke and had to move the fridge to wipe the floor. One of them fell off." He shrugged his shoulders.

"You're kidding," I stammered as I grabbed my throat with both hands.

"Sorry," he shrugged again.

"Geez, Jim!" I wailed once I'd found my voice. "Those roosters are getting very hard to find and are becoming quite valuable. I wish you'd be more careful." I felt moved to scold him for his cavalier attitude about the whole situation.

"Well, the poor bird didn't look very valuable laying on the kitchen floor in a thousand pieces," he chuckled. He apparently thought that was a witty response. I opened my mouth to speak but no words would come. Jim returned to his tires. I walked back to the house rubbing my temples. No doubt he was just as perplexed about my emotional trauma over a shattered rooster as I was about him bothering to put a shine on the tires of his truck.

I put the new rooster with the others, but the glow was gone. I was properly reproached for being so smug about only paying twelve dollars for this fabulous find. And so, my hunt for that fifth and balancing rooster continues. But, alas, I reminded myself, this is the joy of junkin'.

Perhaps I'll be motivated to make another run up to Mount Dora soon. And I would definitely stop in at the Triple M to sit and chat with Jiggy.

Over the next few days we watched as Max settled nicely into his new life. He was eighteen years old and had spent at least the last sixteen of those doing heavy ranch work, working cattle and riding miles of fence in the blistering sun or pouring rain with very few, if any, days off. He was a remarkably sweet horse, but we noticed that he watched us warily—or perhaps it was weari-ly—whenever we approached him in the first week he was with us, as if he were saying, "What do you want from me?" I made a point of going to him several times a day, usually with a carrot or a chunk of apple hidden in a pocket that I carried just for him. He eagerly sniffed me up and down with his adorable heart-shaped nose until he found the treat. And then we would stand together, Max willingly staying by my side. Sometimes I was quiet, and other times I would talk to him about Jiggy. But I always made sure that I did something nice for him, like scratch his back or gently rub his eyes and face. Max would sigh and lay his head against me, and it wasn't very long until he realized that we wanted nothing from him. He was free to be a horse.

Baby Colt

I SET MY HAND ON THE SHOULDER OF THE SORREL MARE and bent down to peer under her belly, trying to get a look at the baby colt hiding behind her legs. Her injured foal kept avoiding me by skittering around to her opposite side every time I walked around the mare. Unfortunately, the gruesome wound on his leg opened up a little more each time he took a step and it was bleeding freely now. On second thought, the bleeding might not be such a bad thing, considering the amount of dirt in the wound; it might clean it out a bit. But rather than upset him any further, I decided to allow him the security of keeping his dam between us, and evaluate him from a distance.

It was clear that the trauma to his back leg was life threatening and would need immediate intervention. I could smell the rotting flesh before I had even gotten close to him. My concern was whether or not the little guy could tolerate being loaded into a trailer and hauled to Proud Spirit, about an hour away.

And I was worried about being alone in this isolated field

Jesse, finally safe at Proud Spirit

with unrestrained and unfamiliar horses. The mother of the injured colt seemed gentle enough. I could sense that she was accepting of my presence. She had stood calmly while I jockeyed back and forth trying to get near her baby.

I was more concerned with the other horses that had surrounded us—a large black stallion and three additional mares, each one with a foal at her side. I quickly checked their proximity. They were a little too close, and I didn't want them to start bickering with each other and have one of them slam into my back while I was bent down and not paying attention. I waved my free arm at them in a swishing motion, the same way another horse would ring its tail in irritation.

The other mares and their babies moved back at my insistence, but the stallion stood his ground. I knew nothing about these horses, what their behavior was like or how much they had been handled. Right now I needed to concentrate on the wounded colt and couldn't risk being challenged by the stallion if he viewed me as a threat. I stood tall as I slapped my arms against my thighs and stomped my foot. "C'mon, you," I said. "Get back now." He bobbed his head at me a few times but then retreated several feet. I faced him squarely and gently waved my arms at him, asking him to move back a little farther. He did, indicating that he was an amiable fellow, and I relaxed my watch on him.

I turned my attention back to the dam of the injured colt and stood once again at her shoulder while I allowed the baby to settle down. The mare gently turned her head back to get a better look at me. "Easy, mama," I said, stroking her red coat. "That a girl. I just wanna help."

She nickered softly as I bent down to visually examine the baby. He watched as my head appeared below his mother's belly. I could hear him on the other side of her, clacking his tiny teeth together the way young horses communicate their vulnerability and innocence. "Easy, baby," I whispered very quietly. "Easy."

He remained where he was, but rocked back on his heels to shift his body and create some distance between us. That was when I saw the severity of his injury. And that was when my heart sank.

I slowly straightened and looked away, blinking rapidly as tears stung my eyes. It is so upsetting to see an animal suffering, and he was just a baby. I took my ball cap off and rubbed a hand over my sweaty forehead as I thought about what to do next. I popped my hat against the leg of my jeans in frustrated anger. "You stupid man," I said out loud to the owner of the horses.

But the man who owned these horses didn't hear a word I said. He wasn't even on the property. He was a stranger to me and had gotten my phone number from a local business that knew about our horse sanctuary. He had phoned me just a few hours previously. I was immediately alarmed the moment the man started speaking. It was only eleven in the morning and I could tell by his slurred speech and disconnected sentences that he was more than likely intoxicated.

"Sumbody tol me you'd take a horse I got," he said.

"Well, what's the situation?" I asked. "Why are you getting rid of him?"

"He got a cut on his knee and I can't take care of it."

"A cut?" I repeated. This seemed like a strange reason to part with a horse. "How bad of a cut?"

"Well, I don't know," he muttered. "I don't know nothin' 'bout horses. But the ol' fella looks pretty bad. And there's stuff fallin' outta the hole."

I couldn't imagine what sort of "stuff" would be falling from the wound. "But why can't you take care of it if it's just a cut?" I asked.

"'Cause he ain't never been handled," he said. "I can't get near him."

"I don't understand," I said. "You have an elderly horse that's never been handled?"

"No, he ain't old. He's a four-month-old colt."

"Four months? You just said—" I began, but shook my head. "Why hasn't he been handled?"

"I didn't know I was supposed to. The mare gave birth and we just ain't never messed with him. Ya see, I was gonna—"

"Okay, listen," I interrupted, wishing to dismiss lengthy explanations. "Is the cut directly on his knee, or above or below it?" I was trying to determine if tendons were involved.

"Well, it's over that whole knee area on his back leg." I noted he said "back leg." That's not a horse's knee, it's his hock, but I decided not to bother with an anatomy lesson. And he said "the whole area." That was possibly a red flag.

"When did it happen?" I asked. "Is it still bleeding?"

"I only just noticed it today. There's a lot of dried blood down on his hoof and it only bleeds when he moves."

Was his hoof bleeding as well, I wondered, but decided not to ask. "Have you called a vet?" I asked instead.

"I been tryin' to get one out here for a couple days. They won't come unless the horse is caught up," he said.

"That's understandable," I replied. "You can't expect a vet to waste time trying to corral your horse. But what do you mean 'a couple days'? You said you just noticed the wound today. When did the colt get injured?" I asked. He responded to my questions, but still nothing made sense. The longer we talked the more confused I became. The only solution was for me to go take a look.

"All right, listen," I said. "Where is the horse now?" The man had told me his name was Robert at the beginning of our conversation and I took down the address to his house where the injured colt and his dam were being kept. "But I won't be here," he told me. "I gotta go do some errands. When you get here, jus' go on through the gate and drive to the back of the property. That's where the horses usually hang out. See what you think about that cut, and then call me on my cell phone and tell me if you'll take him off my hands." I wrote down his cell phone number amid concerns about this guy driving in the condition he was in. "Oh, and make sure you close the gate," he added. "The horses are just loose on the whole five acres."

I pulled off the side of the road in front of Robert's house. He had told me to drive to the back, but I decided to walk. It was only five acres, and after viewing the property I saw that there was so much trash strewn all over I was afraid of puncturing one of the tires on my truck. I turned off the engine and started down the dirt driveway. As I walked along I passed by a mound of beer cans that was literally the size of a Volkswagen Beetle. There were piles of black plastic garbage bags that looked as though they had been ripped open by raccoons. Rotting food and household trash was everywhere. It seemed curious that someone would choose to throw their garbage out in the yard rather than put it out by the road for pickup.

I approached the small, run-down house. It looked as though

at one time a wooden porch had led to the front door. But the deck and railing were now lying in a tangled heap on the ground with nails protruding from them at every angle. A stack of cinder blocks formed a makeshift new set of steps and provided access to the home. Back behind the house there was dangerous debris everywhere I looked. Several rolls of unraveling barbed-wire fencing were lying in the high grass. There was a pile of storm windows leaning against a tree. Most of the glass was broken out, leaving jagged shards. The four-foot-wide mowing decks of several large tractors were flipped over in the weeds with the blades sticking up. And there was no cross fencing, which meant that the horses had access to all this junk. It was a disaster waiting to happen. Although I was about to find out that it already had.

A short distance from the house the weeds were over my head. I followed a worn path used by the horses and went in search of them. I spotted the eave of a ramshackle shed and headed in that direction. The horses weren't there, but it was obvious that this was where they congregated as the weeds were tromped down and the clearing was littered with manure. I could see another path cutting diagonally to the back corner of the property and I started down that way. I finally found them a short distance from the shed, in another clearing under a small oak tree.

I was surprised to find nine horses; Robert hadn't mentioned any others besides the mare and her injured colt. All nine of them lifted their heads at my approach, but none came forward. I quickly noticed that one was a very unremarkable grade stallion who was about two hundred pounds underweight. Standing with him were four very unremarkable grade mares, each with a baby at her side. All of them were thin and had poor coat condition. More than likely they were full of parasites. I looked around at the fresh piles of manure. I kicked a few of them open with the toe of my boot and saw the worms, confirming my suspicion.

I kept my distance from the horses and stood about thirty feet away. I just wanted to watch them for a moment. It was mid-day and hot and humid. The light breeze shifted direction, and suddenly the repugnant odor of decaying flesh came over me like a wave. My work as a firefighter had frequently taken me into the home of a person who had died alone and sadly went undiscovered for days. The smell was unmistakable. I found myself saying a silent prayer that what I smelled was hopefully some woodland creature off in the weeds that had died a natural death, rather than one of the horses.

I scanned the cluster of thirty-six legs, easily separating the babies from the adults until I finally spotted the colt I was searching for. Just as Robert had told me, his tiny hoof was coated in dried blood. I followed the wide line of blood up the inside of his back leg and saw an enormous evisceration. His hide, flesh, and muscle had been ripped from the bone. The wound was equivalent to the size of a large man's open hand. The "stuff" Robert saw falling from the wound was maggots.

"Dammit," I muttered out loud. "He calls this a cut?"

The wound was at least a week old, maybe more. It looked as though the colt had gotten hung up on something sharp and then struggled to free himself, causing the horrific injury. I couldn't imagine the pain this little baby must be in. And I was absolutely furious at the unconscionable neglect. I also noticed that every one of the horses on this property had numerous gashes and lacerations all over their legs in various stages of healing from wandering through all the trash.

I moved in closer and used body language to maneuver among the herd, keeping them at a safe distance. Once the mare and her colt were isolated from the others I managed to get a better look. That was when the baby saw my head appear below his dam's belly and he rocked back on his heels. The movement caused the articulation of the large flexor tendon that runs along the front of the leg. I saw the white sheath of the tendon disappear into the lower half of his leg while the upper half stayed right where it was; it had been completely severed in two. And each time he moved his hoof dirt and bacteria were being pulled into the wound.

I put my cap back on my head and rubbed the mare's neck. "I'm so sorry, mama," I told her. "Your baby is in a bad way."

"Dammit." I spat the word out a second time as I stalked off through the weeds and made my way back to my truck. I grabbed my cell phone and punched in the number Robert had given me to reach him. He answered on the third ring.

"Robert, I'm here at your house." My jaw was clenched as I tried to maintain some composure. It is very rare that I become confrontational when dealing with an abusive or neglectful owner in my work rescuing horses. It's not worth my time. I've also learned the hard way that if someone gets angry, it makes it that much harder to get a horse out of their grasp. I've learned to temper what I say and keep my emotions in check till a horse is in my custody. But I had a gut feeling that Robert would be easily intimidated, and I needed him to be for the sake of this colt. This neglect was beyond inexcusable. What kind of person would let an animal walk around for a week or more in this condition? I was nearly blind with rage.

"Oh, good," Robert said, not suspecting the anger in my voice. "You find the colt? Ya gonna take him?"

"Yeah, I found the colt," I said. "I want you to listen to me. I'm heading home as soon as we hang up, but I'm coming back out here right away with a trailer, just as soon as I can, and I'm taking the colt *and* the mare."

His reaction was instant. *"Whoa! Whoa! Whoa!* You're not takin' the mare. I never said nothin' about you takin' the mare."

I ground my teeth together, took a deep breath, and spoke very deliberately. "I want you to listen very carefully to my words. I'm coming back out here, today. I'm taking the colt *and* the mare. Do you understand me? It's not open for debate, Robert."

"Why ya gotta take the mare? I need her. She's a good brood mare."

I ignored his stammering and continued talking. "We can do this the easy way or we can do this the hard way. Your choice. Either you give me permission to take the mare or I'm calling law enforcement. What's it gonna be?"

"Don't call the cops!" he hollered. "I just got out of jail last summer! I don't understand why ya gotta take the mare. I'm tryin' to make some money breeding these horses." I tipped my head back in exasperation and searched the cloudless blue sky for words. I will never comprehend why people get into backyard breeding with grade horses thinking that they're going to make money. I believe that every horse is beautiful and the lives of all animals are valuable. But to allow indiscriminate breeding between unremarkable horses is detrimental to the entire horse world. I wanted to ask Robert if this was his plan, to make money, why wasn't he at least taking decent care of them? Why wouldn't he feed them proper nutrition and provide them with a safe environment? Not only is this the humane thing to do, at least he would have something viable and worth selling. But I kept those opinions to myself for the time being as I concentrated on getting him to let me take the mare.

"Listen to me, Robert. Do you have any idea how seriously injured this colt is?" I asked. "He is under so much stress right now. I am *not* going to abruptly wean him from his mother and add to his trauma. I don't know if this baby is even going to live. Do you understand what I'm saying?"

"I didn't know it was that bad," he said.

"Have you looked at it?" I yelled into the phone. I lost control. "It's so infected his skin is rotting. It stinks so bad I'm surprised vultures aren't circling."

"Oh, no," he moaned.

"The tendon is severed in two. Maggots are crawling out of it!"

"Oh, please, I—I didn't know," he moaned again. "I swear I didn't know. Look, I can tell you're really mad. Go ahead and take the mare. Just don't call the cops, okay?"

I ignored his last sentence.

"I'll be back as soon as I can with a trailer and someone who can help me load them," I said.

"And I wanna be there, okay?"

"It's your property," I answered and hung up. I immediately called our vet, Dr. Mark Davis. When I reached him I explained the situation and asked if he'd be able to meet me back at Proud Spirit in about four hours. It would be evening by then, but this baby couldn't wait. Mark agreed to come after his scheduled appointments were finished for the day. I jumped in my truck and sped away.

When I arrived back home I went directly to our kitchen phone, grabbed my address book from a drawer and started leafing through the pages. Jim was on duty at the fire department and wouldn't be able to help. I scanned the book in my hands searching for someone who could.

Getting the injured baby was going to be a challenge at best. I hadn't been able to get near him. There was no barn with stalls at Robert's. No paddock areas or corrals. How was I going to convince a severely injured colt who had never been handled to jump into a trailer? That was another problem: We didn't have a trailer. I needed to find someone with infinite horse sense, someone who knew the nuance of every single flick of a horse's tail and the meaning behind every twitch of its ear. But more importantly, I needed someone who would be kind and patient beyond measure. And who had a trailer.

I got all the way to the letter S in my address book before I found the person I was looking for. Or persons, I should say. Larry and Donna Scarson owned a cattle ranch about five miles from Proud Spirit. They probably could have run their operation with just two or three horses. But they had nine. The significance of that is the extraordinary commitment they have for their horses who can no longer do ranch work. Larry and Donna have never pushed their older horses off on someone else. They understand and accept the responsibility and kindly provide the horses on their ranch with a well-deserved retirement.

Donna and I were kindred spirits in many ways, but especially when it came to animals; she never turned her back on one in need. She believed in living simply in order to give more to the world around her. And Larry would call himself "just an old cowboy." He talked tough, but was a big softie with a gentle heart. He was the kind of man that you wanted around in a crisis; he was calm, sensible, and knew when to step in and take charge. And a handshake from Larry was as honorable a contract as could ever be made.

Both Larry and Donna were outstanding horse people. But the best part of all, Larry could write poetry with a rope. And with no way to corral the horses, that might be the only way we were going to get that injured colt.

I dialed their number as I quickly glanced at the clock. It was past lunch time, and too early for dinner. I didn't think I'd catch them in the house. But Donna picked up.

"Oh! I can't believe I got you," I blurted out.

"I just got off the tractor. We've been draggin' pastures all day and I came in for some water," she said. "Is something wrong?"

"Yeah, I've got a little problem. Is Larry home?" I asked.

"He's still out there, but I can get him. What's wrong?" she asked again.

I quickly told her about the colt. "I hate taking you away from your work, but I need your help," I said. "And your trailer."

"You start headin' this way," Donna said without hesitation. "I'll get Larry in, and we'll hook up the trailer and be out at our gate by the time you get here."

I breathed out a sigh of relief. "Thank you."

Larry pulled his truck into the driveway at Robert's. I hopped out of the cab to open the gate. There was no sign that anyone was home, but Larry pulled on through and parked. He and Donna got out and the three of us stood at the back of their trailer looking around and talking about how to proceed.

"There won't be any trouble haltering the mare," I told them. "And obviously, wherever we lead her, the baby is going to follow. The problem is going to be keeping the rest of the herd away from us . . . preventing them from causing a ruckus. And then of course, convincing the baby to jump into the trailer."

Larry scanned the property once more. "I wish there was some sort of corral," he said, then quickly waved his hand. "But there isn't, so we'll work with what we got and do what we have to do." He looked from Donna, then back to me. "Right?"

"Right," we both said. His optimism made me feel hopeful for the first time that day. I grabbed the halter I had brought and the three of us started back into the weeds to find the horses. We found them in the same clearing they were in when I left. Larry and Donna hung back while I easily walked up to the dam of the injured colt and slipped the halter over her head. I turned to lead her up to the front of the property where Larry's truck waited. Her baby looked exhausted, but he lifted his head and slowly limped on three legs to stay with his dam. Larry and Donna were horrified when they saw his wound.

All the other horses shuffled away and seemed unconcerned when I haltered the mare. For just a moment I thought maybe they wouldn't follow us. It would be out of character, but maybe they were all too tired and hungry and sickly to worry about one of their herd mates being led away. I felt bad about their lack of interest, although it would make trying to load the colt much easier. But they surprised me. As soon as we got out of the stallion's sight he hollered for his mare. Then he came crashing through the weeds in a pounding run to find her. And naturally, the rest of the mares and their babies came right behind him—all normal behavior. I just dreaded the confusion with the colt struggling so to even walk.

I stood near the horse trailer holding the mare. Her baby was pacing close by, as best he could on three legs. He was getting upset because he wanted to be next to his dam, but wouldn't come to her as long as I was anywhere near. The rest of the horses were running in a circle, kicking and bucking as they kept an eye on their herd mate. I knew we just needed to stand still for a moment and everyone would settle down. I noticed that the mare appeared unconcerned about her baby fretting. She never nickered in an effort to comfort him. She didn't even look back when he went behind the trailer and was out of her sight. This was heartbreaking to me and I wondered if the awful smell from his wound was going to make her shun him. If she did push him away, he was old enough to survive without her. We just needed to get him home to Proud Spirit to see if he could survive this wound.

The rest of the herd was beginning to settle down. A few of them were picking at the sparse grass. Just then a car pulled up to the gate. A thin man in his mid-forties got out of the passenger side and opened the gate. I assumed it was Robert. The car was being driven by an elderly woman. I was glad to see he wasn't behind the wheel. The woman pulled though the gate and parked up near the house. She got out with some effort and then reached into the back seat for a small bag of groceries. As she started walking towards the house she glanced over to where I stood with the mare. I nodded in her direction and offered a small smile, but she didn't acknowledge me and continued into the house.

The thin man approached. "That's my mom," he said. "I gotta help her get the rest of the groceries in." He stunk of alcohol.

"Are you Robert?"

"Yeah," he said and shoved his hands in his pockets. "Yeah, sorry. Ah—just do what you gotta do." He turned to walk back to the car.

I momentarily felt sorry for the guy. He was a mess. But I returned my focus to the horses. I looked over at Larry. "Let's do this," I said.

I backed the mare up so Donna could open the wide door of the trailer. Then Donna jumped up into the back and I handed her the mare's lead rope. Donna gave the rope a gentle tug and urged the mare forward. The horse stepped into the trailer without a second of hesitation. "That was easy," I said and we all smiled at each other. Donna remained in the trailer holding the mare while Larry and I turned our attention to the baby. But he was about to make his presence known.

He came from around the side of the trailer. We weren't sure what would happen. Our intention was to encourage him to the back, near the opening, where he could see his dam. We hoped that his need to be with her would overpower his fear of us and he'd scrambled in to be by her side. Before he realized where she was he turned in a panic and couldn't see her. He screamed out for her and then frantically turned in a circle. The mare's instincts kicked in and she shuffled around trying to keep her eye on him. Then she answered his call. The baby colt saw her inside the metal beast and he exploded. With all his might he slammed his body against the side of the trailer. My breath caught in my throat. Then he did it again. The sound of his head and shoulder hitting the metal was horrifying.

"Donna," Larry called. "Get her outta there." Donna turned the mare and quickly led her out. She unclipped the lead rope so mama and baby could reunite without our interference, and hopefully the baby would calm down.

Larry took his cowboy hat off and rubbed his hand across his chin. His eyes were squinted in thought. Donna and I looked at each other, but remained quiet. "We need to create some sort of corral," Larry said. "There's enough junk around here, we ought to be able to figure something out."

"How about if we back the trailer up to the corner of the house," Donna offered. "We can open the door and brace it against the house. That will create one barrier. Then we can find something else, something light, to use like a gate and set it up on the other side, but leave it open. We'll get mama near the opening of the trailer and just back off till he comes to her side. Once he does we'll close in whatever we find, like a shoot, so they have no place to go but inside the trailer."

"Good idea," Larry nodded. He got in his truck to back it up while Donna directed him into position, close to the house. I ran around to the back of the property to see what I could find that would act like a gate. I spotted an aluminum extension ladder. Perfect. We could lay it beside the trailer. Once the baby was standing beside his dam at the open back end, all we had to do was keep one end of the ladder in contact with the side of the trailer while we gently swung the other end against the house. We wouldn't actually be in there next to the horses, so hopefully the baby would stay calm. We could ease the ladder closer and closer to them, making the area they had to stand smaller and smaller. We imagined the mare would easily step into the trailer on her own, as calm as she had been so far. And as we encroached on the colt from behind, it would make sense that he would follow his dam. He would have no place else to go.

We got everything set up. I brought the mare to stand near the back of the trailer. The baby became frantic again, even though he could see where she was. And while still upset, he slowly inched towards her. Donna was at the door of the trailer, but on the opposite side, ready to close it once the horses were in. Larry and I had completely backed off allowing the baby time to settle down and figure out that he could stand near his mom.

Suddenly, Larry quietly got my attention. "Mel," he said. "Do you think that fella could help us?"

I shrugged my shoulders. "I suppose. Do you want me to go get him?"

"Well, I'm just thinking . . . as hard as that colt threw himself against the trailer, it might be smart if there was three of us holding this ladder." I went to knock on the door. When Robert answered I explained what we were trying to do, and he came outside with me to take a position on the ladder.

The baby was standing calmly next to his dam. Larry nodded at me to pick up the middle of the ladder, and he asked Robert to take the end near the house. The three of us started closing the gap, swinging the ladder like a gate. Just as we thought, the mare stepped up into the trailer without a backward glance. The baby tried to follow her, but couldn't figure out how to jump up. His front legs crashed against the bumper. We all stopped moving in on him, trying to keep him from getting frantic. But he looked back at us with his eyes rimmed in white, and in a blind panic he turned in our direction and slammed into the ladder.

I could hear Larry holler, "Hold him! Hold him!" And then it suddenly felt like I was bearing the entire weight of the ladder. The end Robert was holding crashed to the ground. I looked over and saw Robert covering his mouth with his hands. He was crying. The baby saw the opening and was gone.

"What the hell—what are you doing!" I yelled.

"Oh my god," he cried. "I swear—I swear I didn't know it was that bad."

"How could you not know, Robert!" I was still yelling.

"Oh my god. Is he going to die?"

"All right," Larry said. "Let's calm down."

"I can't do this," Robert cried. "I can't stand to look at him."

"You're going to do this." I was *still* yelling. "Whether my vet comes here or he comes to my house, that baby needs immediate medical care. And the only way we're going to do that is if we get him corralled."

"Mel, easy," Larry said.

"Jesus," I spat at Robert, ignoring Larry. "Get it together."

We got everything set up again. Then we all backed off to allow the baby access to his dam. He finally came to her side. Just like the last time, we eased the ladder closer and the mare quietly stepped into the trailer. We all took a deep breath and gently closed in the area where the baby stood. His front legs hit the bumper again, and he turned away, but not quite as frantic as the last time.

"Easy guys," Larry whispered. "Easy. Robert, hold your end up and get braced for him to hit it."

The colt turned in a circle and then stopped. We had a perfect view of his wound. It was bleeding, the blood flowing freely. We could see the maggots around the edges. Robert let out a wail and dropped the ladder again.

"Robert!" Larry said.

"Pick it up!" I yelled. "Pick it up, dammit!"

Robert turned his head away and blindly reached for his end

of the ladder. "Open your eyes!" I hollered at him. "If he gets past you . . ." Robert held the ladder, but kept his face averted so he wouldn't have to look at the baby.

"Robert! Move in," Larry said. "But easy."

We inched the ladder closer to the little colt. He circled away from us, knocked into the bumper, and then, miraculously, he jumped in beside his dam. Donna quickly, but quietly, pushed the trailer door closed and set the latch. I saw the relief in her eyes. I shut my own eyes and let the air out of my lungs. I couldn't remember ever losing my temper so badly. And I couldn't remember ever feeling so much relief over getting a horse loaded into a trailer. Donna came to my side and put her arm around my shoulder. She gave me a gentle squeeze. "Let's get this little guy to Proud Spirit," she said.

Larry and Donna got in the cab of their pickup truck. I started walking towards the gate to open it. Something stopped me and I looked back at Robert. He was still sniffling. "You all right?" I asked.

He nodded and once again shoved his hands deep in the pockets of his jeans. "I didn't know he was that bad," he said. I bit the inside of my mouth and slowly shook my head, then offered a little nod. I turned to go open the gate.

I had walked only a few yards when Robert stopped me. "Hey," he said. "Um—if the colt dies, I'm wonderin', can I have my mare back?"

I took my sweaty ball cap off, looked down at the ground, and let out a humorless laugh while I shook my head in disgust. I walked back to where Robert stood. "Man, I don't even know what to say to you," I told him. "I'm not here to pass judgment on you, but you can't even take care of yourself. You've got no business with these horses."

"I can't work. I lost my license. I was gonna make some money selling the babies."

"You're not going to make money off these horses, Robert. Look at them. You're not taking care of them. They're skinny and sick with worms."

He looked over at the horses. "That was a good stallion."

"He'll make a good gelding," I said, softening my tone. "He's just a grade horse, Robert, that's all he is. And he's sick. He might make someone a good trail horse. For someone who can take care of him. But he needs to be gelded. You've got no business breeding with him. Or breeding these mares."

"So I guess that's a no on gettin' that one back," he said as he tipped his head towards the trailer waiting by the gate.

I didn't respond. He knew the answer. I turned and walked away.

Larry, Donna, and I pulled into Proud Spirit. I ran in the house to phone our vet, Mark, to let him know we had arrived with the injured colt. He told me he would be here in under an hour. We led the mare out of the trailer and the baby stayed right by her side. He was exhausted. Donna and I walked both horses into the barn and she helped me get them settled in a stall. We gave the mare some grain and filled the water bucket. I brought in several flakes of fresh hay. While the mare was happily eating, her little colt lay down. They were finally safe and secure.

Larry and Donna had to leave to tend to their own animals. I hugged them both and they headed home. And then I waited for Mark to arrive.

"What do we got, Mel?" Mark asked as he came striding down the aisleway of my barn. That was the routine greeting he always said whenever he came to tend to one of our horses, even if he already knew what I had called him about. I smiled at the sound of his voice in spite of the situation at hand and felt the knot in my stomach begin to ease now that he was here. I stepped closer to the stall where the mare and her baby were resting and pointed in their direction. Mark came to stand by my side and looked over the stall door.

"Hmm." Mark's brow furrowed. "That's not good," he said.

"The flexor tendon is severed right in half," I told him.

"You sure?" he asked. I nodded.

"Well, he could still get around. Wouldn't be ride-able, but he could have a decent life. I'm more concerned with the severity of the infection. Where it's spread to."

I nodded again.

"Is Jim home to help us?" Mark asked.

I shook my head. "Nope."

"Just you and me?" he asked.

"Just me and you," I answered.

Mark lightly sedated the little colt by an intra-muscular injection and waited for him to get drowsy. We managed to get a halter on him now without too much effort. We walked him and the mare out into a grassy paddock off the barn. And then Mark gave him an IV injection that would put him all the way out. The baby colt quietly slipped to the ground.

I kneeled down and put the baby's head on my lap. Mark was ready with a bucket of cleaning solution, sponges, and gauze and began scrubbing the horrible wound on the colt's leg. Next he took out his surgical scissors and started cutting away the necrotic tissue. Mark found the severed tendon and shook his head, but continued working.

"Uh-oh," Mark said.

"What?" I asked.

I saw Mark's shoulders drop and he stopped tending the wound. "Come here," he said, motioning for me to get on the other side of the colt. I gently took his head off my lap and crawled on my knees to where Mark indicated. "What's wrong?" I asked again.

"This is bad, Mel. Let's roll him onto his back." I took the colt's front and back right legs and pulled him towards me. Mark had his left legs. We rolled the baby onto his back, exposing the deep V formed where a horse's rear leg meets its stomach.

All I managed was a sharp intake of breath before I turned my face away. I put my hand over my mouth and started crying. Whatever the baby had been hung up on had caused more injury than we realized. When we exposed this V-shaped area, we found a massive wound much more serious than the one on his hock. His leg was almost completely amputated, internal organs were involved, and he had actually castrated himself. The cavity was full of maggots. I was sick over the pain this baby must have been in. I got up off my knees and walked away, sobbing into my hands.

Mark came over to me and set his hand on my back. I couldn't stop crying. I thought the colt was going to survive this; I thought he was safe. But not now—this wound was too severe. We stood without talking for just a moment while Mark let me cry. Finally he said gently, "I know the answer, but you need to say it." I nodded, but couldn't talk. I made no move to return to the baby's side. "Mel, I'm sorry. But he's going to start waking up shortly," Mark said. "We need to do this. For him." I nodded again and wiped the tears on my face.

We walked back to where the baby lay on the ground. My body felt heavy, as though I were walking through water. I couldn't seem to get my breath. I kneeled down and put the colt's head in my lap once again. I cupped my hand over his eye and leaned down to kiss his face.

"I'm so sorry, little baby," I whispered. "You won't ever hurt again."

My tears fell like a river on the downy soft coat of his cheek. I finally looked up at Mark and nodded. Mark gently ran his hand down the colt's red coat and lowered his eyes for just an instant and shook his head. He placed the needle in the baby's vein, and then connected the syringe with the euthanasia solution. Mark glanced up at me just before he slowly pushed the plunger. I watched the pink drug leave the syringe and then I squeezed my eyes shut and waited for the life to leave this innocent little soul.

"I want you to write a formal report on what you found here," I told Mark. "I want charges pressed against this guy." I got up and went in the house to get my camera. Mark and I documented the wounds the little colt had suffered. I brought out an old sheet which Mark helped me wrap the baby in. We left his head uncovered by the sheet so his dam could still see him and grieve on her own terms.

After we finished Mark went back to the baby's head and kneeled down. We were both quiet, each lost in our own thoughts. Suddenly he looked up at the mare. She had stood calmly nearby the entire time. I saw Mark cock his head to the side and stare at her more intently. He stood up and went to her side. He looked over at me with a small grin on his face, then looked back at the mare.

"What . . . ?" I laughed through the tears still lingering in my eyes.

"Well," he began. "This might either be good news or bad news."

I waited for him to go on.

"I think she's pregnant, Mel."

For just a moment I stared at him with a blank expression on my face. The emotions of the day had taken their toll and I was in overload.

"Pregnant," I whispered. My initial reaction was not a happy one. This horse had been through enough. And in addition to that, Americans send one hundred thousand horses to slaughter a year. We aren't taking care of the ones that are already here and I didn't like the idea of bringing more into the world. I turned my attention to the mare. It suddenly dawned on me that I had barely even looked at her, so focused on the baby as we were. I went to her and ran my hand down her neck. She turned her head to my chest and allowed me to pull her close.

"I'm so sorry you lost your baby," I told her. I realized she needed a name and I leaned back a little to look at her face. Suddenly my heart was in my throat. There was something familiar about this mare. I lifted her chin and moved her forelock to the side. She had a lovely blaze with an odd red spot in the white hair. I took another step back to get a better look. Then I circled her entire body. When I came around to her left side I saw a unique splotch of white down on her stomach. That's when I knew for sure.

"Oh my god," I muttered. "This is impossible."

"What?" Mark asked.

"Mark," I said. "I know this horse."

• • •

I had the photographs of the colt's wounds developed and had several of them blown up to 8 x 10s. I took all the photographs, along with Mark's veterinary report, to a meeting with the deputy who handles agricultural crimes in our county. We clearly had a case of abusive neglect, but as is always the case, I was concerned about the governmental red tape and the time it would take to make something happen. If we intervened right away, maybe we could prevent another mare from getting pregnant. But more importantly, maybe we could prevent another accident like the one that took the life of that baby colt. I made the very difficult decision not to press charges against Robert if he would give up all of the horses on his property. If he agreed, we could move the horses immediately. If he didn't, it would be out of my hands and I would have the sheriff's office step in.

Robert and I met later that same week. I handed him a copy of Mark's report and I showed him the very graphic 8 x 10s of the gruesome evisceration. And then I gave him his options regarding law enforcement. All of this had the desired effect. Robert agreed to give up the horses. He signed paperwork that Mark helped me write up. I told Robert what day I would be back to move them.

I found homes for all three mares and their babies. They wouldn't even be coming to Proud Spirit. I would take the stallion and I scheduled an appointment with Mark to have him gelded. Several friends and I arrived at Robert's on the scheduled date with trailers, just a few days after our meeting. There didn't appear to be anyone home. I told everyone to wait out on the dirt road. I'd start walking the horses up. I swung a halter over my shoulder and headed to the back of Robert's property.

I came upon the mares and their babies in the first clearing, but didn't see the stallion. I continued down the diagonal path that led to the second clearing. I found him. He was lying down and appeared to be dozing in the sun. "Hey, fella," I called out.

He didn't move. I stepped closer, but then stopped in my tracks. I realized that he was dead. I was too late. I tried to find comfort knowing that the mares would very soon be in good homes and their babies would be safe. And the dam of the little colt who died was already safe at Proud Spirit. She would be able to deliver her new baby away from this awful place. But as I looked at the stallion I suddenly felt very, very tired. I slowly went to his side and kneeled down as I cupped my hand over his open eye. I gently pushed his eyelid closed and shut my own eyes. "I'm so sorry," I whispered to him. I stayed with him for just a moment and then got back to my feet and went to lead the mares away.

A Baby for Proud Spirit

"WHAT DO YOU MEAN?" MARK ASKED. He was standing beside the lifeless baby colt we had just covered with a sheet. "Did you know someone who used to own her?" He joined me beside the mare.

"Sorta," I said. I was still wiping the tears from my eyes over the loss of the mare's baby as the enormity began to sink in over our finding each other after all these years. And I had no doubt it was her. Her markings were slight, but they were too unique for this not to be her. I glanced at the lone splotch of white on her side that looked like an intricate lace doily. Then I reached up to run my fingers over the perfect circle of red in the middle of her white blaze. "Her name was Dotty."

• • •

It was the spring of 1999. "Are you Melanie?" I turned around to find myself face to face with a perfectly coiffed women in her mid

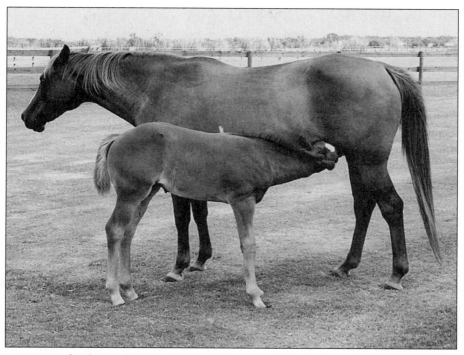

Jesse and Riley

to late sixties. She was wearing expensive clothes and dripping in diamonds. I was pushing a heavily loaded grocery cart through a parking lot and had just unlocked my truck. Before I could answer, the woman pointed at the Proud Spirit logo on my door. "I noticed your truck," she continued. "Are you the founder?"

"Yes," I nodded. "I'm Melanie."

"Do you have a minute?" she asked.

"Sure," I said. "Just let me get this stuff out of the sun."

"This is so funny," she told me while I stowed my groceries in the backseat of my truck. "It's been on my mind to call you for several weeks now. And here you are."

I turned and smiled at her. "What can I do for you?" I said.

"My name is Florence Scott. My husband and I own Scott

Free Farm. Maybe you've heard of—"

"Oh sure," I interrupted. "Of course I've heard of you," I said. "I've always wanted to see your facility. I've been told it's amazing." Scott Free was a renowned Paint horse breeding farm. They stood five spectacular stallions, each one of them a world-class champion. Their stud fee was in the thousands. The farm also owned fifty or sixty brood mares. The get from these stallions sold in the tens of thousands, multiplied by fifty mares a season. Providing they all took. Regardless if ten or so did not, this was a multi-million dollar operation.

Florence smiled at my compliment. "Maybe we can work that out sooner than later. I, um—" she began and let out a small nervous laugh as she twisted one of her rings around a finger. "I have a slightly awkward situation I wanted to speak with you about."

I nodded for her to go on.

"One of our mares recently had a colt that is not saleable. He has no color. And for a Paint farm of our reputation," she laughed again and cleared her throat, "well, that's not a good thing. But actually," she continued, lifting her hand in a dismissive wave, "that's not really the issue. A foal with no color doesn't happen very often, and we can usually get rid of them when they come out like that. There are a lot of people who would give anything to have a baby from one of our stallions—people who would never be able to afford them when they're perfect—so it all works out, and we don't lose any money." She glanced up at me. I nodded again, but remained quiet and waited for her to go on. I wasn't getting a very warm and fuzzy feeling from this lady, and wasn't sure I liked her.

"This particular colt has some serious conformation problems," she said. "My husband wants him put down."

I raised my eyebrows. "Is the colt in pain or unable to get around?" I asked.

"No," she stated. "He's—well, he's ugly. Scott Free Farm does not do ugly. We can tolerate the occasional foal with no color. But my husband wants this horse off the property."

"I see," I said, but I really didn't see. I would never understand this callousness. "And you'd like to know if I can take him?"

She nodded.

"Why don't you sell him or give him away to a good home?" I asked.

"No. We don't think he'll ever be useable. So who would want him? That's why my husband wants him put down," she said. "Or he'd have to go to an organization such as yours. But the only way my husband will allow me to place the colt with you is if you agree not to ever say he came from our farm." She paused for just a moment. "Our reputation, you understand . . . "

"How old is he?" I asked.

"One month.

"When will you wean him?"

"We wean all our babies at three months."

"Three!" I exclaimed. It was just too young. I twisted my mouth to the side and looked off across the parking lot. Lord, I thought, people can be such idiots when their lives revolve around money. I let out a sigh. "Sure," I said. "We can take him."

Florence said she would phone me later, after she had confirmed everything with her husband. And then she invited me to come out to their farm as often as I liked so I could get to know the baby. We said goodbye and I turned to get in my truck.

"He's really not a bad person," she said, stopping me. "My husband, I mean. But you have to understand, this is a business."

On the drive home I pondered all that Florence and I had talked about with a furrowed brow. I did not object to anyone making money from horses. An intelligent and conscientious breeding program is the lifeblood of our domestic animals—dogs, cats, and horses. It is the overbreeding and irresponsible backyard breeding that is in part to blame for so many unwanted horses, and dogs and cats as well, in the United States, and why organizations such as ours even exist. But I got the feeling that everything that came out of Scott Free Farm was nothing more than a product off an assembly line. And that's just as irresponsible as the person who allows grade animals to indiscriminately breed.

I thought about all those babies at Scott Free pulled from their dams at such a young age. I thought about the baby we would be taking and I wondered what he looked like. I started thinking about how soon I could make the hour-long drive to go see him. My gloomy face slowly turned into a smile. A baby! We were getting a baby!

Suddenly I was very excited and I even had butterflies at the thought of it. We had never had a baby before. Naturally, we did no breeding whatsoever at Proud Spirit. The youngest horse we had ever taken in was Wrangler, our little Miniature. But he was already eight months old when he arrived at the sanctuary. This was going to be a brand-new adventure for us.

Later in the week I arrived at the entrance gate to Scott Free Farm. It was indeed an impressive place. I could see four enormous barns, a covered arena, and a reception building. There was bustling activity everywhere. Horses were being led here and there. Workmen were mowing fields and using a weed eater along the fence row. Several mares and their babies were grazing in perfectly manicured pastures.

I read a sign that stated "Please check in at the office" and drove in the direction of the red arrow. A woman looked up from her desk when I knocked on the office door and motioned for me to come in.

"Hello," I said. "Is Florence here?"

The woman looked at me with an odd expression on her face, like she didn't quite know how to respond. "I mean Mrs. Scott." I quickly added. I thought maybe no one referred to her casually as "Florence."

"May I ask who you are?" she said with a friendly smile.

I gave her my name and told her I was from Proud Spirit. "I'm here to see the little colt," I added.

"Oh, yes," she said and stood up to reach across her desk to shake my hand in greeting. "My name is Tara. I'm the farm manager. The Scotts don't really come out here. You kind of caught me off guard when you asked for Flo. I was worried I had forgotten an appointment."

"They don't live on the farm?" I asked.

"No, no," Tara laughed. "It's too dusty out here, too smelly, too many flies, too much farm stuff. If ya know what I mean."

"Mmm," I muttered.

"They have a home on the coast. They only come out here for meetings with certain clients during big sales and the breeding season."

"Ah," I said.

"Follow me," Tara said. "I'll take you out to the colt."

We walked into an open-air barn that easily housed twenty mares and their foals. It was a beautiful building and designed perfectly for dealing with the Florida heat and humidity. There was heavy-duty piping separating the stalls, which allowed for lots of ventilation and a clear view of all the residents. The twenty or so mares and their babies were all standing in deep, fluffy shavings and each stall looked clean and fresh. I was instantly gooey over the babies and I wanted to stop at every stall to nuzzle them. Each and every one was so tiny and so adorable. But Tara was striding on ahead of me without a sideways glance and I stayed close on her heels.

We came to the end of the stalls and Tara turned the corner. "Here we are," she said. There was a makeshift wall of plywood hiding whatever she was pointing to. I poked my head around. The first thing I saw was a sorrel mare, dozing with her head down. I didn't see a baby. Tara stepped back out of my way and motioned me forward.

"There he is," she said.

I finally saw a little patch of red curled up in a corner. The deep shavings had worked over most of his body till he was nearly completely covered over. "Oh my," I breathed as I brought my hand up to my chest. "He's so tiny."

"Yeah, we didn't think he was going to make it," Tara said. Just then the colt lifted his head. His dam nickered to him and he got to his feet. He was much smaller than the other babies in the barn. His head appeared almost half the size of theirs. He was a lovely dark chestnut color with a fuzzy downy-soft mane that stuck straight up. I could feel tears stinging my eyes over how adorable he was.

"Florence said he was ugly," I said. "I can't see anything wrong with him, other than being small."

"Well, I don't think she meant he was ugly, but when you compare him to these guys—" Tara indicated the babies in the other stalls. Every single one of them was splashed with loud color, showing off the superior heritage of their Paint sires. "And he actually has some conformation problems. His legs aren't developed properly. He'll never be rideable."

I stepped forward to pet the mare. "What's her name?" I asked.

"Um, this is . . . " Tara began as she reached out and flipped over a laminated card hanging from the bar. "Oh, that's right," she said when she read the card. "It's Dotty. See the dot on her forehead?"

I reached up and gently moved the mare's forelock aside. There was a perfect circle of red inside the white of her blaze.

"Why are they back here, behind this wall?" I asked.

"We have clients coming to the farm this weekend. The Scotts didn't want people seeing him." Tara turned to leave. "Stay as long as you like," she called over her shoulder. "I've got stacks of paperwork I need to get to."

I nodded and absentmindedly thanked her. I couldn't take my eyes off the little colt. I kneeled down and reached through the bars to touch him. He skittered away from me and leaned against his dam. And then he fumbled around under her belly trying to nurse. The mare cocked her leg so he had better access to her udder.

"What a good mom you are," I said. I stood up and ran my

fingers through her mane. It was full of tangles and knots. I worked a few of them free while the baby nursed. "I promise to take good care of your baby," I told her.

Over the next two months I drove out to Scott Free Farm at least twice a week, sometimes more. I named the baby Fire. "We'll show them," I whispered to him one day. "Crookedy little legs or not, you're going to run like a firestorm, aren't you!" The name Fire stuck and it seemed to suit him. I smiled every time I said it to him. He was filling out, and getting stronger, but he didn't appear to be growing much in height. Best of all, he was no longer afraid of me. When I reached out for him, he came right over. I ran my fingers over his eyes and played with his fuzzy little forelock.

I also spent a lot of time paying attention to Dotty. I felt so bad for her. She was usually very sullen and just stood with her head hanging down. I started bringing her a small bag of baby carrots every time I came. She devoured them happily and then searched my hands for more. It was the only time I really saw her perk up and my heart broke for her. This barn was clean and all the horses were well fed and cared for. But it was a horrible way to live; stuck in a stall all day, every day. Why do so many people ignore the fact that horses need to move? I just would never understand it.

The time was approaching for little Fire to be weaned from Dotty. I somehow got it in my head to speak with Florence about allowing Dotty to come to Proud Spirit as well. I couldn't stand the thought of taking Fire away from her when he was still so tiny. And I had spent the last two months developing a very close bond to her. I groomed all the knots out of her mane and spent hours rubbing her back and legs. She loved being massaged. Both Fire and Dotty had become very important to me. Even if I had to pay for her, I would happily do it to bring this wonderful mare back to Proud Spirit so she could keep her baby until he was a more reasonable age for weaning. And she would be put in a pasture where she could move about and teach her baby to run.

I parked my truck up by the mare barn at Scott Free and headed down the aisleway. This would be one of my last visits before Fire was weaned. I curled my fingers around the bag of carrots that I had brought for Dotty. I came to their little area in the back and peeked around the plywood wall. Their stall was empty. I turned in a circle, peering into the other stalls, thinking maybe they had been moved. They weren't there. I walked to the back of the barn and looked out at the paddock. There were horses there, mares with babies, but none were Dotty and Fire.

"Tara," I said as I cracked open her office door. She glanced up. The look on her face told me she wasn't happy to see me. "Where's Dotty and Fire?" I asked.

"Oh, damn, Melanie!" she sputtered. "I meant to call you." She got up from her desk and told me to come into the office. "Oh, damn," she repeated when I stepped inside.

"What happened?" I choked out.

"Well, relax. It's nothing bad. But someone should have called you." Tara motioned for me to sit down and I shook my head. "I should have called you. A close friend of Flo's came out here a few days ago. Flo had told her about the colt and that we were giving him away. She fell in love with him. Flo let her take him."

My mouth fell open, but no words came. I turned away from Tara and looked out the window in the direction of the mare barn. My shoulders fell as the air left my lungs. I felt like I had been kicked. "I don't believe this," I whispered. My words were barely audible. I shook my head, slowly, trying to find some way to comprehend what Tara just said to me. I finally managed to speak out loud. "I don't believe this!" I realized that my voice was raised and tears were burning my eyes.

"I'm sorry," Tara said, looking everywhere but in my direction. "I tried to object. But you do what you're told around here. And I should have called you. It's just been so hectic this month." She sighed deeply. "I'm sorry," she said again.

"Florence knew how much I had been coming out here! She

knew I named him!"

"I know," Tara said.

"Where's Dotty?" I asked.

Tara sighed heavily once again before she answered. "They sold her," she said.

"What? Why? To who?"

"I don't know who it was. But Dotty wasn't producing color. They sold her and three other mares, dirt-cheap to some guy that's a friend of one of our ranch hands. I wasn't happy about it. He seemed like a scumbag. But like I said, you do what you're told around here."

"I would have bought her. I would have bought them both," I said.

"I'm sorry," Tara repeated.

I turned to the door and put my hand on the knob. "I didn't like her when I first met her." I kept my back to Tara. I knew this wasn't her fault, but I was blaming the messenger. "I doubt she cares, but if she ever asks how I took this news, or ever wants my help again, tell her I said 'go to hell.'" I walked out the office door and let it slam behind me.

• • •

"Mel, this is amazing," Mark said. "Are you sure it's her?"

I didn't stop touching the mare formerly know as Dotty the entire time I was telling him the story of how she and I knew each other. I didn't want to let her out of my grasp.

"I'm sure," I said. "Open her mouth and look at her gums. She has three black spots on her upper gum and two on the lower."

Mark opened the mare's mouth. He bent over to look, and then released her chin. He looked over at me and smiled. "How'd you know?"

"I used to rub her gums when she was in Scott Hell. She loved it. Most horses do, but she really loved it. It would nearly put her to sleep. I'd have to get down on my knees because she'd drop her head so low."

I started crying again. "I can't believe this." I put my hand over my mouth. "I just can't believe she's here. With me. She finally gets to have the life she deserves."

Mark shook his head. "It really is amazing how this came about. But good god, will you stop crying. You've cried enough today to drown a small village." He shook my shoulder and I started laughing through my tears. "Here, think about something else," he said. "Think about giving her a new name. Dotty's gotta go."

I thought for a minute. "How about Jesse?" I said.

"Jesse is a great name," Mark nodded.

We both looked back at the mare. "A baby," I whispered. I reached up and hugged Jesse's head. "A baby you'll actually get to raise . . ."

• • •

On May 24, 2004, Jesse gave birth to a darling little filly. She was a rich sorrel color with a big white star in the middle of her forehead as her only marking. Jim and I were madly in love with her. We determined that she would become a symbol of everything Proud Spirit stands for. A horse does not have to be used to have value. She would never feel a bit in her mouth or a saddle on her back. She would never be in service to man. We named her Riley, as in "The Life of . . .".

To Catch a Donkey

"WHAT'S THAT?" ASKED JIM.

"What's what?" I said absently as I straightened from kneeling down next to one of our horses. We were in the aisleway of our barn tending to Hawkeye, a six-year-old Standardbred gelding. He had come in from the pasture that morning with a cut on his leg. It wasn't serious, and the big horse was standing calmly, but Jim was holding onto Hawk's lead rope for me and gently soothing him by rubbing his neck and forehead as I cleaned the wound.

I turned my attention to Jim and looked up at him questioningly, wondering what he was referring to. "That," he replied with a nod, indicating the smaller pasture at the south end of the property. I turned, my eyes following his gaze out the back of our barn, but I already knew what he was looking at.

"That," I announced, "is a donkey."

"Well, I can see it's a donkey. Is he the one you and Sarah have been trying to catch for a week?"

Biscuit enjoying life at Proud Spirit

I gave him a quick and jaunty nod. "The very same," I said, proudly lifting my chin.

"How'd you finally get him?" he laughed.

Jim had just arrived home a few minutes before from a twenty-four-hour shift at his job as a battalion chief with the fire department. He hadn't even changed out of his uniform when I'd enlisted his help in doctoring Hawkeye's wound. I was waiting till he'd had a chance to unwind from work before introducing him to the newest member of our horse sanctuary: a bedraggled and shaggy donkey whom I had met for the first time just a little over one week ago.

I thought back to that day when I'd been on my way home after making a visit to a local country vegetable stand. It was the middle of March and in Florida that means strawberry season. I had purchased an entire flat of the sweet berries with the intention of using about half of them to make a sauce for drizzling over shortcake, and the rest would be dipped in powdered sugar and eaten like candy.

The Collins family had been farming in this part of Florida for generations. They owned several thousand acres along both sides of a county road. A portion of their land was dedicated to orange groves, watermelons, and strawberry fields, but the bulk of their crops were corn, green beans, squash, and the like. They operated a quaint country store with an adjoining vegetable stand adjacent to their packing house. And there was a small petting zoo on the property as well.

I had stowed my strawberries in the bed of my pickup truck and was driving past the vegetable fields. As I came to a densely wooded area that bordered the Collins farm I noticed a small donkey standing near the fence line. I'm not sure what compelled me to stop, other than the fact that he was just as cute as could be and appeared to be begging for someone to stop and say hello. I couldn't resist pulling over and I parked my truck alongside the dirt road. The donkey lifted his head a bit higher as he stood watching me walk toward him. I noticed that one of his long ears flopped limply to the side, giving him a comical appearance.

"Hey, little fella," I said as I made my way down the ditch. As I came closer, I could see a small amount of blood dripping from a wound on his shoulder. When I first saw him from the road I had no reason to suspect that there was a problem or that he was in any sort of trouble, I simply wanted to pet him. But aside from the wound on his shoulder I could now see that all the hair on his chest was abraded and his skin rubbed raw. There were similar sores across his entire back. His face was bald and covered in bloody scratches, and his ears had lesions where mosquitoes and other biting insects had been eating him alive. I was about ten feet from him and closing the gap between us when I spoke again, in a much softer tone.

"Why, you're a mess," I told him as I reached out with my hand to rub his neck.

He startled me by rearing back and letting out an incredibly loud, screeching bray: *"Eee eee eeeee HAAAW!"* Having been around animals my whole life and living with the thirty-plus horses, one donkey, and the seven dogs we had at that time, I certainly understand that all animals have their own unique voice. But I had never heard anything like this! I stopped where I stood and stared at him with my eyes popping like saucers.

Before I could react any further the little donkey had bolted back into the woods and disappeared from my view. I stayed where I was for a few more moments. I could hear him dodging trees and crashing through the palmetto scrub as he made his escape.

"Geez . . . ," I said aloud at his abrupt departure. I looked up and down the road wondering what I should do. The poor boy clearly needed some care. He had an awful skin infection and had rubbed himself raw trying to relieve the itching. I decided to continue home and phone the Collins family to see if they knew anything about him.

"Is Eddie available?" I asked the woman who answered the phone at Collins Farms.

"He sure is," she said. "Can I tell him who's calling?"

"My name is Melanie," I replied.

"Melanie . . . ?"

"From the horse sanctuary over here in Myakka." I thought this would identify me better than telling her my last name. Eddie was the youngest son in the Collins hierarchy. He and I had met briefly several years ago when I helped him find a pony for his children.

"Hey Melanie," Eddie said when he came to the phone. "How've ya been?"

"Hi Eddie. I'm just fine, thanks."

"What can I do for you?"

"Well, I'm not sure. Do you folks own that wooded area just east of your fields?"

"Yep, that's part of our land."

"I was just at your store about a half-hour ago. On my way home I saw a donkey standing up near the edge of the trees right there."

"You're kidding," he exclaimed.

"Is he yours?"

"Well, he is if it's the one that used to be in our petting zoo. We had several incidents where he bit a couple kids. Nothing serious. But we had to move him, and my brother, Larry, put him over in the woods. But that was at least ten years ago."

"Ten years!" It was my turn to express shock.

"I guess we sorta forgot about him. I haven't really thought about him in a long time and just figured he was probably dead by now."

"Oh, my . . . ," I muttered quietly and shook my head. "Well, he's not dead, but he's covered in open sores. What would you think about letting me bring him out to our sanctuary?"

Eddie started laughing. "If you can catch him, you can have him."

And so this adventure began. "How much land is he on?" I asked as I envisioned trying to round up a donkey that hadn't been handled in ten years.

"That's about forty acres of solid woods. Except for a small area of wetlands."

"Hmm . . . ," I said aloud as I silently wondered to myself how I would ever get him. But I also knew I'd never be able to sleep at night unless I tried.

Eddie gave me the combination to the gate that led to the wooded parcel as well as free rein to do whatever I needed in order to catch the little donkey. After he and I hung up, I phoned my niece, Sarah. She's an accomplished horsewoman and has infinite patience with troubled or difficult animals. I would definitely need her talents. And her trailer, as we'd never had the funds to purchase one for Proud Spirit.

"So what do you think?" I asked Sarah after telling her the whole story. "Wanna help me get this poor guy?"

"Yeah!" she replied. "He really needs some care, and this'll be interesting besides."

"How do you think we should go about it?"

She was silent on her end of the phone for a moment. "That depends on him," she finally offered. "I guess we need to see how he reacts to us. He's pretty wild, huh?"

"Well, keep in mind that he was in their petting zoo," I said, trying to sound casual and downplay the daunting task ahead.

"Yeah, but ten years ago." She laughed at me. "Do you want to just go over there and try to find him? Without my trailer?" she asked. "See if we can even get close to him?"

"Naaaw," I scoffed. "Go ahead and hook your trailer up. I have a feeling this isn't going to be that tough. I'll just bring along some grain and a few apples. I think he's gonna surprise us."

An unreasonable cocky confidence had taken hold of me. I foolishly decided to run with it, even though common sense and the reality of the situation should've had me squelching such grand visions of simply walking up to a feral donkey who hadn't been handled in years.

Sarah was silent once again and didn't comment on my insistence that she bring her trailer as we sat there on the phone listening to each other breathe. I could imagine her twisting her mouth to the side as is her habit when she would like to protest, but decides to remain quiet.

With unbridled assurance I continued to prod her, "C'mon! Think positive. How hard can it be to coax one innocent little donkey into a trailer? He's probably starved for attention! And for something other than pine needles and palmetto fronds. As soon as he gets a whiff of the treats I'm gonna bring . . . ," My voice trailed off as I heard the absurdity of my own words.

"Humph," Sarah finally grunted. But I continued to insist she hook up her trailer and then we decided we'd meet at the gate that led to the woods where our donkey roamed. I packed a bucketful of sweet grain and apples and set it in the bed of my truck, then headed off to bring him home. I hoped.

I left my truck out by the road, but we pulled Sarah's truck and trailer in through the gate. Sarah watched me as I swung open the back doors and left them propped open. I picked up the bucket of goodies and started walking towards the tree line.

"What did you do that for?" Sarah asked.

I turned back to look at her. She was standing with her hands on her hips, her brow knitted together as a perplexed smile spread across her face.

"What?" I said.

She wordlessly tipped her head toward the open doors of the trailer in response. "Well, when we lead him back here with the grain how do you expect him to get in the trailer unless the doors are open?" I replied and continued into the woods. Although there is a sixteen-year age difference between me and Sarah, our relationship is extremely close. However, depending on the situation it can run the entire spectrum from one of best friends and contemporaries to that of aunt and niece, and at times even mother and daughter. And so, with a mother's uncanny radar, I could "hear" her snickering to herself at my retreating back and "see" her rolling her eyes as she trudged after me.

Two exhausting hours later, soaked in sweat and covered with mosquito bites, Sarah and I sat on the edge of her empty trailer staring dejectedly down at our mud-caked boots. My shoulders were slumped as I reached into the bucket that I held wearily on my lap. "Want a apple?" I asked, offering it to Sarah. She glared at me in response. I sighed and dropped the shiny red fruit back into the grain. We never caught a single glimpse of the donkey. Never even heard a twig snap.

As we prepared to leave I convinced Sarah to unhook her trailer and leave it in the little clearing. I wanted to sprinkle the grain I had brought all over the ground near the open doors. I would pour the rest of it onto the floor so the donkey would at least begin to get the idea that this area of his forty acres was a good place to come visit, and stepping up into the trailer would reap rewards. As a final lure, I placed all three apples in a tempting row along the fender of the wheel well.

She acquiesced, and then we agreed to meet early the next morning to try again. The sun was just coming up as we parked out on the dirt road the following day and then walked together to check the back of the trailer to see if the grain had been eaten. I noticed from a distance that all three apples were gone from the fender. And the neat pile of grain on the wood floor was no longer there. "Ah-HA!" I smugly exclaimed, thrusting a fist in the air. "He was here!" I started to move forward to get a closer look when suddenly Sarah's hand shot out and she grabbed my arm, preventing me from taking a step.

"What?" I asked.

"Look," she said, pointing to the ground where I was about to walk.

"What? What am I looking at?"

"What you're looking at," she said, releasing my arm, "is raccoon prints. What you're *not* looking at is donkey tracks."

All over the ground and across the wooden floor of the trailer were perfectly preserved sandy raccoon prints. Not a donkey track to be seen. "Hmmm," I muttered as I scuffed the toe of my boot into the dirt. "You're right." I hesitantly looked over at the fender where I'd placed the three apples. Sure enough, the only things there were fresh scratches in the paint of Sarah's new trailer along with one nasty blob of raccoon poop precariously balanced on the curve of the metal. Rotten little varmints.

Sarah had a sour look on her face as she picked up a stick and flicked the disgusting calling card from her fender. I cleared my throat and then let out a little cough. "Well," I said cheerfully, "let's go find our donkey!" I remained upbeat and struck out for the trees swinging a fresh bucket full of sweet grain.

An hour later we were once again defeated and sitting on the back edge of the trailer. Tromping over pine roots and palmetto scrub is hard work. The muscles in our legs were protesting from the previous day and we didn't have the perseverance to struggle through the entire forty acres again this second day.

"We need to bring food and water for ourselves," Sarah said as she looked at the bucketful of grain I once again held on my lap. I nodded, mightily feeling my thirst. "And we need a new game plan," she continued as she took off her ball cap, wiped the sweat from her forehead, and then gathered her long blond hair back into a ponytail. I nodded once again in agreement, but remained silent. I was pathetically bereft of any solid ideas on how to catch this donkey.

Sarah stuck her cap back on her head and nudged me in the ribs. "You got any ideas?"

"Nope," I said as I tapped my toes together and knocked some of the mud off my boots. "Well," I finally began. "If this was a horse . . . we'd just, um . . . in theory . . . you know," my voiced trailed off weakly.

"In theory? In theory, what?"

"Well, we'd just—you know, we'd . . . it's just that donkeys seem to have their own MO," I muttered lamely.

"Their own MO?" she asked with a furrowed brow. I assumed the query was rhetorical and decided not to answer her.

"I got nothin'," I finally shrugged. "What about you?" I lifted my eyes to meet Sarah's and we just sat there looking at each other. Suddenly my gaze shifted up to her hat. I was immediately transfixed by the embroidered logo on the front of her ball cap. It showed a rearing horse with his hooves pawing the sky. My mind drifted as I envisioned us resorting to the unsavory idea of hiring twenty rough and tough cowboys, all of them riding muscled-up ranch horses. I saw them crashing through the woods, spitting tobacco and bellowing: *"Hya! Hya!"* all while swinging lariats through the air trying to catch this one tiny little burro.

"Are you sure he's even still here?" she asked. "I mean, it's sorta weird that we haven't even seen him, or at least heard him."

I shuddered, closed my eyes for just a second and shook my

head, trying to rid the image of the donkey running in horrified terror from the marauding cowboys. "Oh, he's here, all right," I said, returning to the present. "He's just a cagey little fella, that's all."

The following day we met in the clearing a few hours before sunset. Sarah was well rested with renewed enthusiasm. Mine was waning. "Okay, here's what we're gonna do. We need to flush him out, so let's split up," she offered. "We'll stay on the fence line, but you go that way and I'll go this way. At whatever point we meet we'll veer into the woods from there and cut through the middle." I nodded, pleased that one of us had actually come up with a plan and headed off in my appointed direction.

"Did ya see anything?" I hollered to Sarah as soon as I saw her approaching on the backside of the woods. I could see her shake her head. "Hear anything?" I added. Once again, she shook her head. "You?" she yelled. I too shook my head in the negative. We joined up and leaned against the fence to rest, both of us slightly out of breath. I set the heavy bucket down, took my glasses off and wiped the sweat out of my eyes with the sleeve of my T-shirt.

"We forgot to bring water," I observed astutely. "Again."

"Ugh . . . ," said Sarah, her tongue lagging out of her mouth like a panting dog. "This is crazy," she added. "We need to make this space smaller and confine him somehow."

I nodded in agreement as I stacked my hands along the top rail of the fence and rested my chin. I was looking away from the woods, across the vegetable fields. Suddenly I stood up straight and smacked Sarah on the arm. "Look!" I exclaimed.

She turned in the direction I was pointing as she rubbed her stinging arm. At the end of a long furrowed row there was a stack of rolled up portable fencing. The Collins family used these light weight plastic rolls to cordon off certain fields from the public who came out during the U-Pick season. I would call Eddie and ask him if we could use a few of them to limit the area our elusive donkey could roam.

We decided to set up the fencing in the next day or two. With more clarity for reaching our goal we started making our way back through the center of the woods. The sun was beginning to go down, but with determined steps we walked a few yards, our knees bouncing high as we navigated the tangle of palmetto roots and fallen limbs. Then we stopped to peer into the dense brush and listen, our eyes keen as we searched for any movement ahead of us, our ears sharp for any sound. If only we had some idea of where he was! But the only sound we heard was that of our own ragged breath. Unfortunately, that was very soon drowned out by the unnerving buzz of mosquitoes rising up from the forest floor.

There is something ecologically wrong with the fact that one must contend with mosquitoes in mid-March. The ones in Florida must be mutants. We had been slapping at the irksome insects every time we ventured into the woods. But with the encroaching dusk the air around us instantly became agonizingly thick with them. Unless you personally witness this eerie onslaught, it can only be described as something out of a Stephen King novel. We quickly abandoned our donkey quest and made a break for the clearing, both of us waving our arms like mad women. In the wild frenzy of trying to keep the loathsome blood-suckers out of my ears, eyes, nose, and mouth I had inadvertently hit myself on the head with the bucket of grain. Rather than risk being knocked unconscious I decided it would be wiser to unburden myself and I flung it, grain and all, unceremoniously into the brush.

We made it back to Sarah's truck. We sat with the engine running and the air conditioning blasting, staring out the windshield with renewed determination for getting our poor little donkey out of these bug-infested woods. Sarah had a full schedule at work the following day and would not be able to meet me to help string out the fencing to resume searching for our donkey, providing Eddie would let us use the rolls. And that was exactly how I had begun to think of him—as ours. He no longer belonged to the Collins family. And I was now unwilling to walk away from this in failure. However, I decided to take a break the following day and stay away as well.

The fifth day of our donkey quest broke hazy with more humidity than normal. It was an oppressive morning to say the least. Before leaving to meet Sarah I decided to bake up a can of Pillsbury buttermilk biscuits so we had something substantial in our stomachs for the task ahead. As soon as they were out of the oven I quickly wrapped them in a double layer of tin foil, folded a hand towel over them, and stuck the package in a paper bag. I wanted them to stay warm. I also remembered to bring a cooler laden with ice, soft drinks, and bottled water.

Sarah and I met in the vegetable field and loaded six rolls of the portable fencing into the bed of my truck. I had spoken to Eddie the day before and he said to help ourselves. He must have been feeling sorry for us as he didn't ask too many questions when I told him why I wanted them. Sarah and I drove back to the clearing and unloaded them at the tree line. "Hey," Sarah said as we set the last one down. I looked over at her. She stuck the toe of her boot in the dirt and shoved her hands into the pockets of her jeans. "I need my trailer this weekend. I'm gonna hook it back up and take it home today when we finish running this fence."

"What!"

"We aren't going to get him today."

"Oh, ye of little faith!" I exclaimed.

"Ye of misguided faith," she mumbled. "It's going to be enough work putting this fencing up. And I have plans to meet some friends and go riding."

With that she turned on her heel and went about closing the doors, securing the latch, and reattaching her trailer to the back of her truck. "Humph," I grumbled.

I reached into the cooler and grabbed each of us a bottled water. We both took a long pull. "Let's eat those biscuits I brought before we start stringing this fence," I suggested. Sarah nodded and hopped up to sit on the tailgate of my truck. I joined her, clutching the bag that was holding the biscuits. They were still warm as I set them between us and unfolded the double layer of foil. "Mmm," sniffed Sarah. "Yummm," I agreed. I handed her one, then broke my own in half and let the steam drift away.

We were happily munching on the biscuits when suddenly we heard an urgent rustling from deep within the woods. "What's that," Sarah asked. "I don't know," I answered as I scooted off the tailgate. The sound was getting closer. "Could it be—?" I breathed out, not daring to believe. As if on cue, an ear-shattering, screeching bray came rippling through the trees. *Eee eee eee HAAAW!*

In a shimmering flurry of dancing palmetto fronds and flailing pine boughs the donkey came skidding to a stop at the edge of the trees. He was slightly out of breath, his right ear lolled and bobbed limply as he swiveled his head from side to side searching for something. Suddenly he had a bead on Sarah, who was still sitting on the tailgate, and he screamed out another bray in her direction. *Eee eee eee HAAAW!*

"Holy crap!" Sarah hollered. "He looks crazed!" Her eyes were wide and rimmed in white as she stared at the apparition. She dropped the biscuit she was holding and slowly slid off the tailgate, not taking her eyes off the maniacal little donkey. Holy crap, indeed, I thought. We both remained stock still, immobilized at the very sight of him.

The donkey took a few shuffling steps forward then lifted his nose to the wind. His nostrils were twitching like the beating wings of a hummingbird. The biscuits, I thought. He smells the biscuits! The realization jolted me from my stupor. "Listen," I hissed through clenched teeth. "The trailer doors. Open the friggin' doors!"

Sarah slowly eased backwards toward the trailer, never taking her eyes off the donkey as her hands searched frantically behind her trying to find the latch. "Now what?" she whispered once the doors had been swung wide.

"Here," I cried out as I stuffed the biscuits back in the paper bag and threw them at Sarah. She snatched the bag from the air and almost simultaneously shot me a questioning glance. "What am I supposed to do with these!"

"That's what he wants," I growled. "Toss them in and move away!" She quickly shook the biscuits onto the floor of the trailer and we both retreated around either side.

The donkey loped forward without hesitation, took one tentative sniff of the trailer floor and then bounded in like a gazelle and immediately started to devour his reward. Sarah and I advanced at the same time and gently but quickly pushed the doors closed with a solid and satisfying resounding clank of metal on metal. The donkey glanced back at us ever so briefly, decidedly unconcerned, and resumed eating our breakfast. We both stood as if in shock for a moment or two, and then burst out laughing.

• • •

Jim stood with his foot perched on the bottom rail of our fence, his elbows resting along the top. "That's quite a story," he said nodding slowly as he watched our new donkey grazing peacefully with three of our horses and our other donkey, Cleveland Brown, named in honor of Jim's beloved home state of Ohio.

"Quite a story? It's unbelievable!" I exclaimed. "Who would've thought—biscuits!"

He shook his head in wonder, looking back out to the pasture. "So what did you name him?"

I cocked an eyebrow and gave him a playful little grin that said, "isn't it obvious," and then I looked out toward the pasture where Biscuit the donkey now happily resided.

Sammy Comes Home

I SLIPPED THE HALTER OVER THE HEAD of the big bay Standardbred gelding. I couldn't bear to look him in the eye, even tough he was blissfully unaware of what was about to happen. I still could hardly believe it. We were standing in the aisleway of our barn. I dropped the lead rope to the concrete floor, I reached up to wrap both arms around his neck and bury my face in that perfectly cozy hollow spot that is formed where a horse's neck joins his shoulder. "I'm so sorry, buddy," I told him. "There's nothing I can do." My voice was strained with emotion as I told my beloved Sammy goodbye. "You will always be a part of our family," I said. "I will never forget you. Ever." He turned his head into me, almost as an embrace, and nibbled on the back of the waistband of my jeans.

Jim and I made the decision long ago that we would never adopt our horses out. When a horse came to us, he came to us for life. I had no reason to believe that this would not be the case with Sammy when the sheriff's office brought him to Proud

Sammy back home with his friends at Proud Spirit

Spirit exactly one year ago. I believed he would be with us forever as I settled him into our family, completely ignorant of what would happen just one short year later.

Sammy belonged to a man who lived on a small rural farm with very few neighbors nearby. The man did some welding in a shop adjacent to his barn, and he ran a few cattle on his thirty-acre parcel of land. He was surrounded by larger cattle ranches and a few small horse farms. Sammy was the only horse the welder owned. The tall gelding first made himself known to the surrounding community when he had escaped from his own property and was found grazing on the front lawn of Shelly and Bill Alton, neighbors who owned a house about one mile from the welder's barn.

Shelly and Bill didn't recognize the horse. Their first thought was that someone had simply driven out to the country with the poor creature they no longer wanted and dumped him off. Shelly and Bill had several horses that they enjoyed for trail riding. They moved the stray to the safety of a paddock and then called law enforcement. Shelly gave the deputy a description of the horse and added that he was underweight and his feet had been seriously neglected. They also told the deputy that they were experienced horse people and would take care of him until an owner or a solution could be found.

A few days later the deputy called them back. Shelly answered the phone. He told her he had located the horse's owner and gave her the man's name and address. Shelly knew the house, but had never met the owner. The deputy asked Shelly if she still wanted law enforcement involved, or would she and Bill just like to handle contacting the horse's owner on their own.

"Well, I'm concerned about how thin he is," Shelly said.

"We discussed that with the owner," the deputy said. "He said that the horse has been missing for about a week and must have gotten down from wandering so long."

"I don't know," Shelly mused. "It's the middle of summer. To get to our property all he did was wander through lush pastures, and there are plenty of ponds. It's not as though he wouldn't have anything to eat or drink. This horse looks neglected if you ask me."

"Do you want to file a formal complaint?" the deputy asked. "Either way, the horse has to go back to his owner even if we are going to investigate."

Shelly thought about it for just a moment. "No," she said. "Maybe I'll walk the horse back home myself so I can meet the guy first. We don't even know him."

Shelly walked the horse up the driveway that led to a modest but well-kept home. She was heading in the direction of a large barn when a man came out of a nearby outbuilding.

"Sorry about the trouble," he called out with a friendly wave.

Shelly smiled, "Oh, he was no problem." She reached up and ran her hand gently down the horse's neck.

The man drew closer. "Deputy said you'd be bringing him back. But you didn't have to do that. I'd've come get him," he said as reached to take the lead rope from Shelly's hand. She let it go and opened her mouth to speak. She was going to say that she didn't mind walking him home. But she never got the words out. The man jerked the gelding around with a whip of the rope. Then he snatched his cowboy hat off his head and smacked the horse across the face with it. The horse threw his head in the air, blinking rapidly as he tried to back away from the man. Shelly's mouth dropped open in shock. The man heard her sharp intake of breath and saw the look on her face.

"Oh, I didn't do him no harm," he said and let out a small chuckle. "Dumb animals, can't feel nothin' anyway." He set his hat back on his head.

Shelly took a few steps back, as well. Her brow was furrowed in concern. "I don't think he deserved to be hit," she said. "Especially on the face."

"You a horse expert, are ya?" the man said. He narrowed his eyes at Shelly, although his tone of voice was still very friendly.

"Well, no. I—" she began.

"Oh, I know," he interrupted, waving a dismissive hand in the air. "There's lotsa talk nowadays about all this fancy trainin'. But I've had horses all my life and I get along just fine doin' things the way I always have."

"What's his name?" Shelly asked, nodding at the horse. She saw no reason to argue with this man. It would be more productive to remain neighborly.

"Well," he laughed and spit on the ground, then ground the tobacco juice into the dirt with the toe of his boot. "My wife named him Glory. Seems like a stupid name for a gelding. But that's what she wanted. I just call him 'the bay.' "

When Shelly returned home she looked in the phone book and found our number. She and I had never met, but she knew about Proud Spirit and our dedication to horses. She called right away to ask my advice.

"I like the way you handled everything," I told her. "There's no reason to become confrontational. You get nowhere. Especially with someone ignorant enough to think animals can't feel pain."

"Is there anything we can do for him?"

"Unfortunately, it's not illegal to hit a horse. Unless it's considered 'severe.' And then it would be your word against his. You'll have to concentrate on the neglect. From your description I don't think he's thin enough for law enforcement to intervene, as stupid as that sounds. Your only option right now is watch out to make sure he doesn't decline further. If he does, call the deputy. Or, another option; you can go over there right now and offer to buy the horse."

Shelly did try to buy the horse named Glory. The man would not part with him. He said that the horse really belonged to his wife. He further explained that she had recently divorced him and moved out of state. Shelly tried to convince him that if his wife had abandoned the horse, then the horse was his responsibility and he could do as he pleased. But he refused to sell.

Over the next few months Glory escaped three more times, each time finding his way to the Altons' house down the road. He was more than likely seeking their lush grass and the company of their horses. Bill and Shelly would wake up in the morning to discover Glory happily grazing in their front yard. And as the weeks went by, the horse had declined more and more. He was seriously emaciated now and the Altons called law enforcement.

An investigation was under way. During a lengthy deposition the man admitted, almost proudly, that he was starving the horse on purpose in retaliation for his wife's leaving him.

The horse was immediately confiscated and placed in our custody. It was a hot and humid summer day when he was brought out to the sanctuary. I easily recalled how he unloaded from the trailer that day, like nobility, his regal head towering above my own as he calmly surveyed his new surroundings. We renamed him Sammy and I had every reason to believe that Proud Spirit would be his home for the rest of his life.

Oddly enough, this morning was very much like the one when Sammy came to us just over one year ago. It was not yet noon, but it was already sweltering, and the sky was such a deep blue it appeared almost purple. The agonizing difference was that today, Sammy was being taken from our fold. Jim came walking up behind me as I quietly shed tears into the strong horse's neck. He put his arm around me and gave me a little squeeze.

"They're here. They're just coming up the drive," he said heavily.

"Oh god, Jim," I cried. "How can they *do* this!"

"They don't have a choice," he said. He let his arm slide off my shoulder and reached over to put his hand on Sammy's chest, and then scratched up and down his long neck. "Sorry, pal," he told the horse. "There's nothing we can do."

Two days ago Jim and I had received a call from the agricultural deputy at the sheriff's office. He told us that he had bad news. Sammy's original owner, the man who had abused him and starved him, had regained custody of this beautiful gelding, and the horse was to be returned to him immediately. All the court proceedings were complete. The abusive owner had complied with everything that had been required of him.

I was stunned, and then livid. I do not believe that someone who is capable of vicious animal abuse actually ever changes. There's something wrong with the internal wiring of their soul. They have no sense of right or wrong and community service simply is not going to fix this lack of conscience. Saying they are sorry does not make it so. And promising to properly care for an animal does not ensure it will happen. It was inconceivable to me that Sammy would be taken from us and returned to this man. To me, they had just handed this horse a death sentence.

My hands were shaking and I felt as if I were being pulled

into a black hole as the deputy told me they would be out this weekend to take Sammy.

"Isn't there anything I can do?" I pleaded. "Would he sell him to us?"

"Actually, I already presented that to him, Melanie. I knew you were going to be very upset about this. And I'm sorry, I really am. I know how attached you get. But he refused to consider selling the horse. Me and another deputy will be out to your place this weekend to get him."

In the blink of an eye, before I'd even had a chance to absorb what was happening, they were here to do exactly that.

I pulled Sammy's face down closer to my own. I looked into his liquid brown eyes and he returned my gaze with complete trust, as yet unaware of how the diesel truck rumbling down our long driveway with a trailer in tow would affect him.

"Listen to me," I told him desperately through my tears. "You will always be my boy and I will always love you."

I turned my face and hugged his beautiful big head to my chest. He willingly rested there as I placed a hand over his eye. His lids went soft and he gently sighed while I held him close, trying to regain some composure.

"I'm so sorry, Sammy, this shouldn't be happening," I told him quietly. "This is your home. This is where you belong." I leaned away from him and looked into his eyes. I knew there was nothing I could do at that moment. I also knew, without a doubt, that I would not give up on this horse.

I heard the din of the pickup truck as it pulled up near the barn, the slam of doors being pushed closed, and then voices as Jim greeted the two deputies. The three of them walked into the barn where I stood with Sammy. I couldn't look anyone in the eye, including Jim, and kept my back to them.

I swallowed hard and looked down at my boots while I held onto Sammy's lead rope. I thought about what he was returning to and my emotions overwhelmed me. I wanted everyone else to be as emotional as I was. I could feel the three men staring at my back, but I didn't turn around. The moment was awkward and nobody said anything.

I suddenly felt very angry and I couldn't seem to get my breath. Dammit! I thought. How could this happen. Jim was my hero. He always took care of everything, he always made things right. Why wasn't he doing something now? Why wasn't he fixing this? And the two deputies—I wanted to yell, "You stupid idiots!" at them. They had seen this through from the beginning. They knew what this horse had been through. Why were taking him back to that hell. "What is wrong with all of you," I wanted to scream.

But instead I started sobbing. Jim stepped forward and put his hand on my back. "C'mon," he said. I shook his arm away. I couldn't shoot the man who tried to starve Sammy to death. I needed to vent my anger on someone and it happened to be poor Jim.

I led Sammy past the deputies and out of the barn, but I stopped just short of the trailer. I would not walk him up to its door or ask him to load. He trusted me and I would not have him believe this was something I wanted. I was not doing this to him.

The deputy stepped forward and reached for the lead rope. I pivoted and placed myself between him and Sammy. I hugged the horse's powerful neck a final time and through my tears I whispered, "People suck, buddy. They really suck." I stepped backwards till I reached the end of his lead rope, and I let it slip from my hand. I turned away and walked into the house without looking back. I felt as though I had been kicked in the stomach and I would not watch him leave our property.

The next few weeks I was consumed with grief. Sammy was on my mind constantly and I worried about his well being. One day I recalled something the deputy told me when they first brought Sammy to us. My heart lifted with hope as I dialed the phone. I left a message for the deputy to call me back as soon as possible and then paced by the phone till it rang.

"Do you remember what you told me in the past about a

facility being reimbursed for caring for a horse while an abusive owner is being investigated?" I asked.

"Yeah," he said. "What are you—"

"Don't you see?" I interrupted. My heart was racing as I spoke. "Sammy was here for a full year. I have all the receipts for a year of feeding him grain and hay, getting his feet trimmed, veterinary care. Everything! All of it!"

"Well, I'll be darned," the deputy said. "Why didn't any of us think of that?"

I felt out of breath. "That guy owes me three or four thousand dollars!" I shouted with laughter.

"Slow down. We need to do this right. That seems a little high."

"You've forgotten about boarding him here for a full year at a premium rate. This is a premium place, ya know," I said. "He owes me four thousand dollars. Might even be five. If he can't pay it, the horse is mine. That's what you told me."

Two weeks later the same deputy came chugging back down our driveway in the same diesel pickup truck, pulling the same trailer. This time when he handed me Sammy's lead rope he included all the legal paperwork proclaiming the big beautiful bay Standardbred gelding a horse who belongs to Proud Spirit.

Ivory Pal

"WELL C'MON OUT TO THE BARN and meet Ivory Pal." Rafael Valle released my hand from his friendly grasp and motioned for me to follow as he turned away. He was a strikingly handsome man in his late thirties, fit and athletic-looking, with captivating eyes that were so dark they appeared almost black. His distinctive accent revealed his Latin heritage and I would later learn that he had been born in Nicaragua.

I had just arrived at Rafael's home outside Ocala, Florida, where I planned to spend a few days with him and his wife, Stefanie, and their champion Tennessee Walking Horse stallion, Ivory Pal. I was there at the urging of a mutual acquaintance of ours named Teresa, to learn more about the wave of humane training methods that was finally, slowly, starting to make its way through the multi-million-dollar Tennessee Walking Horse (TWH) industry, a group with a dark history of employing decidedly shadowed and controversial training practices to get their horses to perform in the show ring.

The ongoing debate is all centered around "The Big Lick" and the duplicity of supportive politicians, wealthy owners, and high-dollar trainers—people who supposedly love this breed and how they "go," even referring to them as the "Pride of Tennessee," while at the same time subjecting them to documented abuse so brutal that horses have literally died from the pain. The enormity of it all is abysmally hard to comprehend. The "Pride of Tennessee" indeed.

Several weeks prior to meeting with Rafael, I had made a short trip up to the Volunteer State. The Tennessee Horse Council was hosting a large expo at their new facility, the Miller Coliseum, and I decided to purchase vendor space in the hopes of garnering attention for my first book, *The Horses of Proud Spirit*. Unfortunately, while I was there I witnessed a disturbing scene involving a horse trained to perform "The Big Lick," and upon returning home to Florida I subsequently wrote an article citing the negatives in the TWH industry, which was published in an equestrian magazine. Teresa read the article and wanted me to see what she and a group of deeply committed individuals were doing to bring about change in the gaited horse world. It was then that she suggested I spend time with Rafael and Stefanie.

• • •

I had never attended an expo before, either on my own or in the capacity of representing our horse sanctuary, so I really didn't know what to expect. But I spoke to several different women involved in organizing the event in Tennessee and was impressed with how friendly and helpful they all were. Just about every discipline and breed of horse would be showcased during the three-day event and large crowds from all over the country were expected to attend.

The drive up was a welcome respite from my normal routine and I enjoyed the change of pace. Equally pleasant was the change of climate. Florida seems to go from really hot, to just hot, and sometimes the temperature even goes down to not so hot. Running to my truck from the hotel room that first morning in Tennessee and actually seeing my breath was quite a novel treat.

I easily found the road that led to the coliseum and made my way through the town of Murfreesboro. Along the way I was properly wowed by the explosion of blossoms on all the Bradford pear trees that lined the streets and dotted nearly everyone's front yard. It was gorgeous! The Miller Coliseum was impressive as well. The grounds and buildings were immaculate. The parking lot was easy to navigate and everything was accessible. I had arrived rather early the morning of the first day, and after setting up my booth I decided to walk around and meet some of the other vendors before the doors opened to the public.

Just about everyone I spoke to was very pleased with the placement of the vendor booths. We were set up in the main building on the top floor ringing the arena where the majority of the events would take place, and we would be able to watch all the horses and riders from the back of our booths. Being unfamiliar with the general routine that takes place at an expo I hadn't given this much thought, but I was told that most of the larger venues around the country put the exhibitors in a separate building and you never have an opportunity to watch the horses performing in the events. I was looking forward to everything getting started.

My life with Jim revolves around the sanctuary and we are immersed in horses. But it is more along the lines of caretakers. We do not show horses, we do not breed them, nor do we make money from them. And in doing rescue work it seems you're exposed to the worst of mankind. So I was truly anxious to get a glimpse of this other aspect of the equestrian community and watch the athletes, both horse and human alike.

Everything imaginable was represented at the event, including world-class trainers putting on mini-symposiums. It was fun watching Josh Lyons, the son of renowned trainer John Lyons, working in complete harmony with his horse. There was a genuine willing partnership; the horse was relaxed, his eyes were soft, and it was clear he wanted to be near this talented young man. Not only were Josh's communication skills with his horse excellent, but he was just as good with the audience. A winning combination of treating our equine companions with the respect they deserve and getting that same message across to their owners.

I was purely mesmerized by the stallion showcase. Too often the horses who arrive at Proud Spirit are elderly and/or neglected, even emaciated. Their muscles are usually slack and their coats dull. To see these stunning, enormous, and powerful stallions, their coats glowing with good health, was spellbinding.

However, I have to say that for me the highlight of the entire weekend was the demonstration put on by The Heinz 57 Hitch Team. They travel and perform all across the country and those eight pure black Percherons are absolutely magnificent. And the gentleman driving them was incredible. He demonstrated how nineteenth-century horses had to maneuver delivery carts through narrow crowded streets and back into alleyways to turn around. It was a fascinating demonstration, and what an astonishing talent that driver had to handle all those reins and keep the horses so cohesive.

I also enjoyed the breed showcase. It was certainly fun and interesting to see the versatility of each group as they came out one by one: Appaloosas, Quarter Horses, Arabians, Miniatures, Saddlebreds, and Paso Finos, to name just a few. I had been especially interested when the emcee announced that the next group coming out to the ring would be the Tennessee Walking Horses. I have several different friends who own Walkers. The immense pleasure they enjoy with this breed on trail rides is well known in our circle. When my close friend Charlena goes into that amazing, gliding running walk on one of our rides with her beautiful mare, Kay, I can't help watching them with awe.

The first horse and rider to come into the arena during the TWH showcase was a young lady dressed in western garb. She was a lovely rider and expertly demonstrated the magical natural gaits that are unique to this breed while the emcee described each gait transition to the audience. Next, out came a sharply dressed gentleman leading a spectacular black horse on foot. The animal walked calmly at the man's side and appeared alert and interested in his surroundings, traits that seem to be so marvelously innate in Walkers. I couldn't hear exactly what the emcee was saying about this particular horse, and then all of a sudden I couldn't really hear anything that was going on around me at all.

I had caught some lurching movement out of the corner of my eye and turned to look at the disturbing spectacle as the next horse and rider came into the ring. I was watching from the back of my booth and for just a second, like the sounds that seemed to have faded around me, the sights became a murky blur as well and all I could see were the whites of this poor horse's eyes.

Naturally, over the years I've read about the controversy surrounding The Big Lick. And of course I have seen photographs and news clips of this decidedly bizarre practice. But I've never stood thirty feet from the nightmare this horse was going through.

I was also under the impression that with the passing of the Horse Protection Act by the United States Congress in 1970 the abusive training practices used to achieve The Big Lick had been eliminated. Apparently, I was wrong. In an instant my entire weekend was ruined and it was also the reason I was prompted to write the disparaging article.

Horse and rider were coming around the ring now. I stepped out of my booth and moved to the rail, watching them through squinted eyes as though it physically hurt to look at them; I swallowed hard and pushed down my emotions. It was like a train wreck—you want to look away from the horror, but you can't. The rider was an attractive young woman and she wore a deep royal blue tailored suit in a rich silky fabric. A matching top hat was perched jauntily atop her head. It was adorned with one big bow at the back and the gossamer ribbons streamed elegantly behind her.

Unfortunately, the pretty outfit became obscene next to the tortured horse who stood out in stark contrast to the other Tennessee Walkers in the ring that day. The horse was fitted with four-inch-high pads on his front feet and heavy chains, or "action devices," were linked around his pasterns, forcing him into an exaggerated distortion of the breed's otherwise beautiful natural gait. His weight was unnaturally rocked back on his hind end, like a dog trying to sit down as his rider pushed him into a canter. I couldn't imagine how difficult it must be for the horse to even move like this, let alone run. The horse was sweating profusely as he lifted his front feet higher and higher to achieve The Big Lick he had been trained to perform. His eyes looked wild as though he were trying to get away from the pain inflicted by the chains as they banged against the sores on his pasterns. The very essence of everything that is beautiful about horses comes from their natural freedom of movement. But this whole scene was just grotesque.

"Oh my god," I muttered under my breath and shook my head in disgust. There was a woman standing beside me and she turned in my direction when she heard my mumbled protest and saw the look on my face. "I'm not a horse person," she told me, stepping closer and lowering her voice. "But I don't understand that. It's ugly." I nodded somberly, readily agreeing with her, and saw that her eyes reflected the same sad outrage I felt as we both turned our attention back to the ring and watched the woman in blue come around. As horse and rider drew near I heard the woman beside me groan, "Ugh, I can't even watch," as she abruptly turned and walked away.

I stared out to the ring and looked into the rider's eyes trying to glean some answers there. Although I knew I would not find them on her face, for it was not her being forced into this disturbing display, it was her mount. I couldn't help but wonder what manner of beast would be proud of the hideous destruction of this remarkable breed's natural gait? What sort of arrogance would someone have to possess to participate in, or even promote, what The Big Lick is forcing on these horses?

Obviously, every discipline in the equestrian community has its share of problems. The horses in American Quarter Horse Association (AQHA) Western Pleasure classes, for instance, look ridiculous with their noses dragging on the ground, but at least they don't look destroyed by torture.

And then there are the bigger issues: the racing industry running colts and fillies way too young to endure the stress and destroying their legs, unwanted American horses going to slaughter by the thousands, Premarin farms, the gross mismanagement of our wild mustangs by the Bureau of Land Management (BLM); while one may be vehemently opposed to the very existence of these industries and/or their programs, at least we understand *why* they were started. The topics all stir up controversy, to say the least, but they can be debated in a somewhat reasonable manner, from both sides.

But this, The Big Lick—the cost to these horses from this abuse goes beyond the depths to which any human being should plunge in the name of money, greed, and politics simply because the base cruelty of it is singularly without explanation.

I'm paraphrasing here, but I believe Mark Twain said something relevant and fitting to this situation: "The fact that man knows right from wrong proves his intellectual superiority over other creatures. The fact that he does wrong to these creatures proves his moral inferiority."

• • •

And this was why I had come to Rafael's home after my first-hand encounter with The Big Lick: to meet someone with a different perspective. Someone who understood the wrong being inflicted on these horses. He was a man on a powerful mission to prove that winning in the show ring could be accomplished without being cruel and I wanted to learn more about him.

Rafael Valle was born in Nicaragua and raised in Miami. It's as though he came into this world loving horses, or at the very least knew they would be his destiny. When he was around five years old he recalls daydreaming that one day he would ride Pegasus. When he bragged about this to his older sister, she told him that the mythical horse didn't exist. Young Rafael cried, but somehow refused to believe her and he clung to this dream throughout his early childhood. And while he would never have a horse of his own when he was growing up, Rafael developed a genuine and lasting connection to them by riding Andalusians on his uncle's working cattle ranch. He also always knew in his heart that one day he would have one of his own.

After their marriage and establishing successful careers in Miami, Rafael and Stefanie decided the time was right to make that dream come true. They made plans to relocate to the Ocala area and buy a small farm, and then begin their search for a few horses, preferably in that order.

But a young Tennessee Walker stallion named Ivory Pal had other plans. The Valles always envisioned that they'd end up with Andalusians; that was the breed Rafael was familiar with and that was where his connection to horses was. A Tennessee Walker was the last thing on his mind—until an ad about a horse for sale in a local paper caught his attention and he went to look.

The TWH training barn had a "creepy" feel to it. All the horses had a lost look in their eyes from too much confinement to their stalls and the painful traditional method of training this breed for the show ring. They looked "shut down," Rafael would later recall. But off to the side he saw a golden Palomino. "He was like a glowing light in this dark and depressing barn," Rafael told me. When he asked about the three-year-old horse the owner of the barn only said that he was a "show reject." He lacked the distinct gaits of a Walker and would never be good for anything but trail riding. The horse was weak and underdeveloped from being stalled 24/7. His feet were almost ruined by the destructive pads and shoes. Rafael left the barn but couldn't stop thinking about the young Palomino.

Rafael Valle and his beloved partner, Ivory Pal

For how do you explain that once-in-a-lifetime connection to an animal that reaches all the way to the center of your heart? It wasn't that Rafael felt sorry for him; there was a barnful of horses to feel sorry for. And how many people go looking for that connection, but don't find it because the horse is the wrong color or the wrong breed or they simply don't listen to their heart? It was possible that one hundred other potential buyers walked by that horse and brushed him off as useless.

The list of reasons they shouldn't have bought Ivory Pal was long and convincing; Rafael and Stefanie hadn't even purchased a farm yet. They dreamed of owning Andalusians and a Palomino Tennessee Walker was the last thing on their minds. And everyone they talked to about the horse ridiculed them for even thinking about buying an underdeveloped "show reject." But buy him they did. And when Rafael got the three-year-old home he did the one thing that probably saved Ivory Pal's life—after removing the destructive shoes, he turned him out and just let him be a horse. Training would come later. Right now Rafael wanted the young stallion to have the freedom he desperately needed to move about and run and develop his muscles. And he wanted some time to forge a bond.

Rafael spent day after day just simply spending time with his new horse without expecting anything from him in return. He brushed him and groomed him, all while talking softly and taking the time to gently offer a comforting rubdown.

• • •

I was parked in the driveway up near Rafael's house where we had just introduced ourselves. I pushed my truck door closed and followed him across the lawn to his immaculate and well-maintained barn where, he told me, he had just given the now seven-year-old stallion, Ivory Pal, a bath. Rafael rounded the wide doorway ahead of me and I saw him gently reach up and quietly say, "Hey, there's someone here to meet you."

I noticed the water and soap suds swirling around on the concrete floor of the wash rack before I could see the horse. I had already seen pictures of Ivory Pal and was aware that he was a very striking golden Palomino. And it was easy to see from the pictures that he was extremely athletic and well put together. I also knew how much Rafael loved him. He had written me numerous letters and we had talked on the phone about the horse several times. I actually felt like I already knew Ivory Pal, so I really wasn't anticipating any surprises when I finally had the opportunity to meet him in person.

But Rafael could have written me a thousand glowing letters about this horse and he never would have prepared me for what I saw, or felt, when I stepped into that barn. Rafael started to speak by way of introduction, "This is . . ." but he didn't finish his sentence when he saw the look on my face. It seems I barely noticed Rafael as he moved slightly to the side.

The big stallion had his head down, relaxed and dozing after his bath as the water still dripped from his shimmering white mane. When I came into view it struck me that he didn't lift his head the way most horses would when a stranger approaches. In fact, he actually brought his chin just a little closer to his chest, elegantly arching his massive neck at the same time as he almost imperceptibly lifted his shoulders higher, drawing himself up. And then, ever so slowly, as though he had all the time in the world, he tipped the top of his head just the slightest little bit to look me directly in the eye.

I lowered my head and stepped forward, drawn to him as anyone who loves horses would be. He was remarkably calm and gentle, and moved with such awareness of his surroundings. I wouldn't have said he was especially tall, yet he seemed enormous to me, but I believe it was more his demeanor than his actual stature. I reached up and laid my hand on his neck. "Hey, handsome," I whispered. He leaned down at the sound of my voice and softly blew his breath in my face. I returned the gesture and there was not a single solitary doubt in my mind that I was in the presence of greatness, and as foolish as it may sound, I felt a little breathless. But it was not his beauty that took my breath away, even though Ivory Pal is one of the most astonishingly beautiful horses I have ever seen. It was more along the lines of those anthropomorphic intangibles that practical people hate. For coupled with his greatness there was a profound benevolence about Ivory Pal that put him in a caliber rarely seen. I stared into his eyes and could actually see my reflection there. I was overwhelmed by the *dignity* that emanated from this horse.

I briefly glanced back at Rafael. "He's extraordinary," I said as I returned my attention to Ivory Pal and ran my fingers through the horse's mane. "And I don't really mean his looks," I added, slowly shaking my head. "It's the air about him." I looked back at Rafael. "I've never felt anything like it."

Rafael nodded and reached forward to touch his horse. "I am blessed to have him," he said.

A few years after bringing Ivory Pal home, after months of

just letting him be a horse, Rafael Valle used a fair and gentle hand in combination with intelligent training methods and natural horsemanship and took the little "show reject" on to win countless blue ribbons and trophies. Remarkably, Ivory Pal is the only horse to win Horse of the Year from Friends of Sound Horses twice, in 2004 and 2005. He was also United States Southeastern Grand Champion for 2004 and 2005. And Ivory Pal went on to win High Point Champion in 2005 at the North American Gaited Horse Championships.

The compelling partnership between Rafael and Ivory Pal has been demonstrated in every show ring and discipline imaginable, including dressage, jumping, performing without a bridle, trail obstacle, barrel racing, pole bending, dance routines to music, and traditional rail classes. Anyone lucky enough to witness what this man and his horse share will be changed forever. But one of the most significant things about this story is that in TWH shows where the "traditionally trained" horses suffer through with heavy pads, chains, and chemicals that distort their gait, and long shank bits that cause pain, Ivory Pal was shown barefoot (an unusual thing to see in any discipline of showing horses, but especially Tennessee Walkers), and he wore nothing more than a simple snaffle bit, and Ivory Pal was *winning*.

"But it was never about accumulating awards," insists Rafael. "Shortly after purchasing Ivory Pal I attended a TWH gaited show, just as an observer. There was a 'sored' stallion there and I couldn't get the horrific sight out of my head. I became inspired to try to make a difference, for all horses, and so we set out to prove that winning could be accomplished another way."

And prove it they did. Rafael and Ivory Pal moved and inspired everyone who ever saw them perform, both spectators and other competitors alike. In 2005 Rafael made the decision to retire Ivory Pal from the show ring. However, the golden Palomino stallion is just beginning a second career. He is an ambassador now, not only for Tennessee Walkers, but for all horses. "We made our point," Rafael explains. "We demonstrated to the entire equestrian community that you can go into the show ring, *win,* and still have respect for these horses. Now we are traveling around and performing in exhibitions just so he can entertain his many fans."

One of the things that Rafael enjoys more than anything is meeting people who tell him how moved they are by the obvious bond between him and Ivory Pal. And a monumental highlight was when a stranger came up to him after a recent performance and told him with tears in her eyes that "it looks like you're riding Pegasus." It seems that childhood dreams do come true.

¡Abrazos Rafael!

• • •

Author note: "Soring" is a term used in the TWH industry. This is a barbaric procedure where a trainer will use various chemicals to intentionally cause sores and/or create sensitive skin on the pastern, the area just above the horse's hoof. During a show chains or "action devices" are placed around the "sored" area to irritate and intensify the pain. This extreme pain causes the horse to lift his front feet higher and higher and lean back on his hind end as he tries to get his own weight off his front end. This is the desired "action" that is referred to as "The Big Lick" at Tennessee Walking Horse shows, and the more "action" the more the crowds in the stands who support this abuse will cheer and applaud.

I would encourage anyone who is interested to read Eugene Davis' *From the Horse's Mouth.* This is an astonishingly brave book that offers a powerful revelation about the hideous truth behind the multi-million-dollar Tennessee Walking Horse industry. These horses are touted as "The Pride of Tennessee," but in my view, as long as The Big Lick exists, in *any* form, the entire state of Tennessee should be ashamed of itself. And the entire equestrian community should be outraged.

Rusty

and Cosmina

FOR NEARLY TWENTY-FIVE YEARS THE PEOPLE OF ROMANIA were brutally dragged into economic deadlock and social isolation from the rest of the world under the Communist rule of Nicolae Ceausescu. The megalomaniac leader squandered huge amounts of money borrowed from Western credit institutions to pay for grandiose palaces and elaborate construction projects. He ordered entire villages razed, and historical churches and thriving business districts were leveled to make way for these dramatic schemes. While the dictator and his family lived in luxury, his countrymen barely subsisted as Ceausescu's government attempted to pay off the enormous debt by exporting much of the country's fuel, as well as its industrial and agricultural production.

In December of 1989 the violation of human rights and forced austerity ultimately triggered an uprising of the Romanian people. In a tide of subversion, the entire Romanian army joined the revolt against Ceausescu. The corrupt leader and his wife were arrested by a provisional government. In a matter of weeks, they

Cosmina giving Rusty a kiss

both were tried and executed.

This is only a tiny overview of the atrocities and irrational actions Nicholae Ceausescu inflicted upon his people and the country of Romania. My purpose is to provide an introduction to a young lady who was born in Bucharest, only an infant during the time of Ceausescu's removal from power, who would later touch my life.

The revolution in December of 1989 brought renewed hope to the people of Romania. Unfortunately, it would come too late for Elena Stroia. The thirty-four-year-old mother of three had just lost her husband to pneumonia. In the weeks following his death she paced back and forth in the sparse one-room apartment they lived in trying to stay warm as she avoided the hungry eyes of her children. Even though the creation of jobs and a strong workforce was burgeoning, these opportunities were primarily put in place for men. And it would take months, perhaps years, to bring about responsible government programs that would help families in her situation. Elena was desperate.

She made the decision to push her sixteen-year-old daughter into marriage with an older man who had already expressed that he would be only too happy to feed and clothe the young woman in exchange for cooking, cleaning, and sharing his bed. Next, Elena considered her nine-year-old son. He would be able to contribute to the larder by stealing and hustling on the streets and eventually gaining employment when he came of age. The boy would not be a burden.

Elena's weary eyes fell upon her tiny three-year-old daughter who sat swaddled in blankets on the cold bare floor. Little Cosmina looked trustingly up at her mother through sooty black lashes. In a hopeless act of survival, Elena gathered the child in her arms and numbly walked several blocks in the biting winter wind to wait for a bus. Forty minutes later she disembarked in front of an orphanage. She quietly filled out the required paperwork while the child squirmed on her lap. After she signed her name, she rose from the chair and handed her daughter over to the director, and then stoically turned to leave. For what would be accomplished by crying and clinging to the baby, she pragmatically told herself. What other choice did she have? Without a backward glance Elena Stroia walked out the door and never saw her baby girl again.

In the years following the revolution orphanages throughout Bucharest were overflowing with children, mostly girls. Families kept their sons for the same reason that Elena did. They could work.

These orphanages were set up to house the children according to their age. With the influx of infants in the late '80s, children were moved as often as every two years to accommodate the impoverished institutions. Over the next eight years little Cosmina, and thousands like her, were transferred from one age-appropriate facility to the other. Finally, when she was nearing twelve years old she was placed in an orphanage where she would more than likely remain until she was eighteen, at which time she would be put out on the street.

The morning of Cosmina's twelfth birthday she was brought into director Alin Petrescu's office. As the young girl came in, her demeanor was polite, yet somehow still exuberant as she sat down in the chair facing his desk. The director quickly glanced at her and could not help but ponder; if ever there was a case study for nature versus nurture, this child was it. She had only been under his care for less than a year, but she had already made an enormous impression on Alin.

Like all of the orphans at his facility, her short time on this earth had been rife with struggle. Feeling cold was more familiar to these children than feeling comfortably warm. The gnawing hunger in their bellies never went away. Most were unable to recall the nurturing embrace of any adult. They had no personal possessions, no toys, no books, not even a hair brush . . . everything was communal. They had nothing to call their own.

But there was something different about this child who sat in front of him now. Above all the others in his care, Cosmina possessed a radiant light that was hard to define. A glow seemed to emit from her very being. Her eyes were always shining and she woke each morning with an enthusiasm for life that should not have been there. There was no reason for it to be there.

Alin Petrescu and his wife had no children of their own. They lived in a small annex off the main hall of the orphanage. He took his position seriously. He was a decent and fair man. But the stress of trying to care for so many children in conditions that were primitive at best had hardened him.

"Well, Cosmina," he began as he looked up from the endless paperwork on his desk. "What would you like for your birthday?" He already knew what she would say. Shoes. They all wanted shoes. And warm socks. Alin glanced back down at the papers on his desk. "Hmm?" he encouraged the child without looking up and blandly waited for her response as he continued filling out government reports.

With innocent self-confidence Cosmina sat forward, looked intently at his down-turned face and firmly told him, "I would like for you to find me a family."

He was startled by her answer and the scratching of his pen momentarily ceased, but then he quickly recovered. "Humph," he grunted as he collected the stack of papers off his desk and tapped them neatly together. "And just how am I supposed to do that? Hmm?"

Alin rose from his desk and turned his back to the child. The gunmetal gray of his filing cabinet matched the December sky outside his window. He tugged open a drawer, the rusty track made an awful sound, and began putting papers away. "You are too old," he flatly stated without turning around.

"But you will try?" Cosmina asked. For a moment the only sound in the room was the *swish-swish* of her bare feet swinging back and forth across the dull linoleum floor.

The director pushed the drawer closed. He stared out the window for just a moment and took a deep breath, and then turned to face Cosmina. He offered her a tight smile. How could her eyes hold such hope, he wondered. In all this despair where did this light come from?

"I will try," he nodded. "I will try. Now, go on with you and join the others," he added, waving her away. She sprung from the chair and turned to leave. "Wait, wait!" he called. Cosmina stopped. "First look through that box there to see if a pair of shoes has arrived from the nuns that will fit you."

She nodded and plopped down beside a cardboard box behind the director's door. He clasped his hands behind his back and faced the window once more. He could hear her shuffling through the second-hand shoes. "Ya!" she laughed. When Alin Petrescu turned around he saw the skinny young girl proudly holding aloft a pair of battered loafers that she apparently thought would fit. She stood to slip them on. "Ya!" she laughed again. They fit.

Cosmina lifted her hand in a wave and turned to leave, to return to the common room of the orphanage. The director listened to her steps gaily dancing down the hallway in her "new" shoes. "Happy birthday, Cosmina," he quietly said to her back as she disappeared around a corner.

• • •

Robert James Brent, RJ to his friends, was a fellow firefighter assigned to the same station as Jim. RJ was newly married, and he and his wife, Kim, had just purchased their first home near the elementary school where she worked as a teacher. Starting a family was deeply important to the young couple and they had discussed their plans for children before they even said their wedding vows. They were eager to have a child of their own, but once they were ready to expand their family, both agreed that their second child would be adopted.

RJ and Kim were very aware of, and grateful for, the blessings in their lives and they were inspired to share these gifts with a child less fortunate. To them it was as simple as that. But life has a way of changing plans. After months of trying, neither was prepared for the findings of their physician when she told the young couple that they would be unable to conceive.

Typical of RJ's upbeat, positive outlook on life, he announced to Kim, "Instead of adopting one child, we'll adopt two."

And so, although it was several years sooner than they had anticipated, RJ and Kim began researching adoption agencies. They allowed their strong faith to guide their resolve and accept this change of plans. The excitement over bringing a baby into their lives filled their home.

It was during this time that American television, newspapers, and magazines were inundated with the shocking conditions of orphanages in many newly liberated Communist countries.

Moved by the reports, RJ and Kim steadfastly turned their attention, and their search for a child overseas. They eventually concentrated on the country of Romania.

Ivan Dratka was a liaison for the Romanian government's adoption program. He had boundless energy that translated itself into an optimism for hopeful families. He was cheerful and always believed that the right things would happen. Ivan became RJ and Kim's contact person in Bucharest, and he would very soon become their friend.

After months of guiding RJ and Kim through the exhaustive paperwork they finally received a call from Ivan. "Congratulations," he laughed through heavily accented English when RJ picked up the phone. "Ivan!" RJ said. "How great to hear your voice."

"You as well, my friend. I'm calling to let you know that a large packet is on the way to you," he said. "Inside you will find twenty-five profiles, along with photos of each of the babies." The paperwork was all in order; they had approval from the Romanian government and the time had come for RJ and Kim to choose a child. They anxiously awaited the package.

RJ had arrived home from work before Kim the day an envelope peppered with international stamps was sitting in their mailbox. He hurried into the kitchen and emptied its contents. Then he took each picture and one by one laid them in a row along the counter. The papers spread its entire length and then spilled onto the kitchen table. RJ slowly walked back and forth along the counter and then circled the table. He suddenly became overwhelmed.

He stared at the eyes of each one of the abandoned babies and stood transfixed, till he forced himself to move on to look at the next one. He almost imperceptibly shook his head. "How do you decide . . . " he whispered to the tiny faces staring back at him.

There was a video tape included in the package from Ivan. RJ left the photographs in the kitchen to go put the tape in the VCR.

"Greetings Kim, RJ!" came the disembodied voice of Ivan as the camera bounced along a barren gray hallway. RJ smiled when he heard their new friend's cheerful voice. "I know we discussed an infant for the Brent household—" Ivan continued. The view showed double swinging metal doors, and then the toe of a scuffed athletic shoe appeared and vigorously pushed open one of the doors. "However, I thought perhaps I would, how you say, slip this in," Ivan said.

The camera swung around to show a large open room. The walls were unadorned concrete. The floor was bare. No curtains hung from the industrial-style jalousie windows. A small grouping of battered tables and a few couches were clustered in the middle of the room. White stuffing protruded from the numerous rips and tears in the pea green vinyl upholstery. Approximately thirty young girls were gathered together on or around the furniture.

Ivan spoke to the girls in his native tongue. A few of them squealed and hid their faces as Ivan laughed at them from behind the camera. Others nervously twisted their fingers together, or wrung their hands as they avoided looking into the device. Two of the girls jumped up and ran for the other side of the room. Most of the others giggled wildly and began chattering away vying for Ivan's attention.

RJ listened to Ivan's gentle tone of voice as he cajoled and comforted the girls. And then he was speaking in English again. "Kim, RJ, I wanted you to meet a few of my country's forgotten souls. These young ladies are told they will never have a family because they are too old and people only want the babies." The camera now slowly moved from face to face.

RJ leaned forward and rested his elbows on his knees, his hands clasped tightly together in front of him. He watched as one black-haired little girl with shining eyes plopped back on the couch and playfully dropped her arm around the shoulder of another. And then suddenly, she sat up and made a face at the camera and burst into tinkling laughter. RJ smiled in spite of the heavy feeling in the pit of his stomach as he looked at the girls and their living conditions. The camera stayed just a moment longer on the girl with the shinning eyes. "This is Cosmina," Ivan was saying through a smile in his voice. "She is our clown, endless cheer from this one. And very smart!" Ivan asked a question in Slavic. The child he called Cosmina answered him. "She tells me she has just turned twelve," Ivan relayed.

Later that night Kim sat down on the couch and began leafing through the photographs and reading each baby's brief profile. She appeared overwhelmed with the sadness of it all. There were so many of them! And it wasn't even the beginning of how many actually needed a home. Ivan could have sent them hundreds of photos, even thousands. She didn't speak, but finally looked up at RJ through the tears glistening in her eyes. "I know," he said. He sat down beside Kim and reached for her hand. "Ivan also sent a video tape," he told her. "I've already watched it."

"Are you sure I want to see it?" Kim asked cautiously.

"Yeah," RJ answered as he nodded his head and reached for the remote to start the VCR. "Yeah, you do."

When the tape ended RJ turned to face his young wife. "I want to try to adopt Cosmina," he said without hesitation.

Kim opened her mouth to speak, but no words would come. The child would be close to thirteen years old by the time all the final red tape was complete. She stared down at the photographs on her lap. What about the baby they'd always dreamed of bringing home? A flood of emotions raced through her mind—but suddenly, all of it quickly settled in her heart, and she knew, the way one instinctively knows that the sun will rise tomorrow, that the impish girl on the tape would one day be her daughter.

RJ had only been home from Romania for one week when he phoned to ask if he could bring Cosmina out to see our horses. "Of course," I told him. In the months between the adoption being finalized, but before RJ flew to Romania to bring her home, he and Kim had written to Cosmina hoping to learn more about her interests. And they asked if there was anything she would like RJ to bring her for the long plane trip back home to America. Their new daughter told them that she loved horses. She said there was a very old, tattered and torn book about horses at the orphanage and she greedily stared at the faded photographs every chance she got. To her, they were the most enchanting animals on earth. Would it be possible, she wanted to know, to somehow see a new book about horses. One that was not faded.

The day that RJ and were talking on the phone I asked him if Cosmina had ever been around horses. I was ignorantly envisioning some sort of excursion to the country that the orphanage might have taken the girls on.

"No," RJ told me. "She's never seen a live horse, not even off in the distance standing in a field. She's never even seen a good picture of one. But it's all she talks about."

"That's incredible," I muttered. "I wonder how she became so intrigued."

"I don't know, but she actually sleeps with that book we got her. Won't let it out of her sight."

"How is everything else going?" I asked. "Is she adjusting to all the changes?"

RJ explained how he and Kim were marveling at Cosmina's personality. They had been warned, over and over, to expect a daunting adjustment period, perhaps even a problem with spiraling emotions, and rightfully so. Cosmina's life, and the lives of other children like her, had consisted of one stark institution after the other. To be suddenly bombarded with the abundance of comforts her new home offered would be overwhelming. Aside from the basics so often taken for granted—a warm bed, a change of clothes, colorful curtains on the windows—something as simple as walking into a grocery store would be a culture shock. A typical American family brought home more food in a month than some Romanian families saw in an entire year before the revolution. And then add in all the extraneous "stuff" we fill our homes with and it could possibly become dizzying. But Cosmina was thriving and she was elated at everything.

RJ told me about his first meeting with Cosmina in Romania. They had several days before the flight home to America. RJ wanted Cosmina to know her people, to understand where she came from. They walked around Bucharest as he showed her the historical sights of her homeland, things she had never seen. Through sign language and gestures they had an amazing day together and formed a deep bond. They finally sat down at a small outdoor café to eat lunch. RJ handed her a menu and indicated that she could have whatever she wanted. Cosmina spoke to the waiter in Slavic. RJ had no idea what she had asked for. When the waiter returned he set a large Coke in front of Cosmina, along with a heaping bowl of strawberry ice cream. RJ smiled as his daughter took several spoonfuls.

After a moment she looked up. Her deep dark eyes were unwavering as she smiled into RJ's. And with the same self-assured confidence that she told director Alin Petrescu that she wanted him to find her a family, she now looked at her new father and told him, "I . . . am . . . happy." Each word was punctuated with a decisive nod. It was her first sentence in English.

Before she had met RJ and Kim, Cosmina had tentatively asked them for a new book about horses, hardly daring to dream that such a thing would actually belong to her. But very shortly she was going to be surrounded by horses. The day had arrived when RJ was bringing Cosmina to Proud Spirit to meet our herd. RJ tried to explain to her through the language barrier where he was taking her. She seemed to understand that Proud Spirit was a place for horses that needed a home. He explained it further by telling her that some of the horses were old and some were injured. But when he told her she would be able to touch one, she lifted her shoulders in a show of bewilderment and shook her head in disbelief. This was inconceivable to Cosmina. She simply could not grasp the concept.

An hour before they were expected to arrive I went out to the gate that opened to our largest pasture. My eyes fell on Rusty and

I went to bring him into the barn. I wanted to introduce Cosmina to one of the horses in the peaceful quiet of the stable without the entire herd jockeying for our attention. More one-on-one.

Rusty was a small breed of horse called a POA, which stands for Pony of the Americas. This is a terrific breed of Appaloosa that has spots over the entire body. He previously belonged to a close friend of ours, a single mom who was unable to keep him. She didn't want to sell him to an unknown fate and risk losing track of the little horse, so we brought him to Proud Spirit for her and welcomed him into our sanctuary. He was a remarkably gentle little guy and would be perfect for a young girl to love on.

I saw RJ's car turn into our driveway and watched from the paddock. I noticed he drove along very slowly, probably allowing Cosmina time to absorb the lush pastures dotted with the nearly thirty horses we had at that time. I couldn't imagine what must have been going through her mind. I walked back around to the barn to greet them as RJ led Cosmina up to the aisleway.

"Cosmina," RJ said, "this is Melanie." I smiled at RJ, and stepped forward to take Cosmina's hand, but then stopped short when I saw the look on her face. The child didn't even see me. And I don't believe she heard a single word that RJ said.

The young girl slowly moved past me, inching closer to Rusty with the caution with which one approaches a coveted dream about to be lifted away by the wind. With each step her eyes grew wider and wider, and her mouth slowly fell open in awe. I saw her chest expand as she silently took in a deep breath and held it, not daring to breathe. When she was about five feet from the horse, her eyes flickered over to RJ as though she were searching for confirmation that this was real. He nodded at her and she finally let the air out of her lungs in an airy laugh.

I had moved to stand beside Rusty. I touched his big jaw and gently turned his head to face her. "Cosmina, this is Rusty," I said quietly.

She turned at the sound of my voice, and appeared almost

startled to see me standing there. Our eyes locked briefly and then she looked back at the spotted horse now standing less than three feet away. "Roosty," she breathed out.

Ever so slowly she reached out to him with her left hand, and then quickly pulled it back as though she'd been burned. She encircled her left hand in her right one and her eyes darted back in my direction. And then that airy laugh again.

I laughed along with her and nodded, encouraging her to go ahead and touch him, but remained quiet. Once again her left hand reached out for the gentle gelding's neck. The moment she made contact with Rusty's coat her breath caught in her throat. The serendipity of a pure miracle was reflected on her face.

For the next twenty minutes Cosmina was lost in bliss as she stroked Rusty's neck and cooed to him in her own language. She put her forehead against his and batted her eyelashes against his nose. She giggled and sighed, and kept looking at her father to shake her head in complete wonderment. The entire time Rusty stood calmly and gently nuzzled her in return.

Cosmina suddenly became thoughtful and looked out the back of our barn. She seemed to be thinking about how to word something. "Um—they," she began as she waved her hand towards the pastures. "They are—ah—hurt?" She took a few limping steps to demonstrate.

"Yes," I nodded. "Some have been hurt, some are . . ."

Cosmina nodded vigorously, stopping me, pleased that we had understood each other thus far. She quickly walked back to Rusty's side and looked at me intently.

"Roosty—" she began, setting her hand on his neck without taking her eyes from mine. "Why?" She patted his neck, and then pointed to the ground. "Why here?"

I looked over at RJ and could feel tears stinging my eyes. My meeting with Cosmina had become fairly emotional for me. I couldn't help thinking about all the horses we had taken in over the years and all the reasons they were here. The abuse and neglect most of them had endured, others forgotten or abandoned by previous owners. The lack of commitment, and the way people use them up, get all they can out of them, and then callously discard them. But here was this young girl from an orphanage in Bucharest who, I've no doubt, considered herself the luckiest child on the planet to simply be in the presence of a horse. And somehow the powerful innocence of that moment brought everything down to a very uncomplicated place.

When she asked me why Rusty was here at Proud Spirit, all I managed was a lame, "Um . . ." And then I swallowed hard. "Well," I tried again, "his family could not take care of him." I looked over at RJ and took a deep breath. We smiled at each other for encouragement.

Cosmina stared at me for just a moment and then turned back to the horse, her brow furrowed in thought. We all were silent. She reached out and once more placed her left hand on Rusty's neck at the same time that she brought her right hand up to her own chest. She slowly nodded her understanding. "Like me," she whispered. "Like me."

I was trying so hard not to cry and looked up at RJ as I wiped my cheeks. I saw tears in his eyes threatening to spill. "But now," Cosmina continued, blinking rapidly as her own tears fell from her sooty black lashes, "now . . . we . . . are . . . happy," she nodded enunciating every word. And then Cosmina wrapped her arms around Rusty's neck and buried her face in his mane. "Oh, Roosty," she laughed through her tears, "I luff you."

Ranger

"WHEN ARE YOU GOING TO WEAN HER?" My guest, an experienced horsewoman, nodded in the direction of the little filly who was snuggled under her dam, eagerly nursing. I marveled at how superbly disposed foals were for this activity, even though it looked like an impossibly awkward undertaking. They spread their gangly legs to all four points of the compass to lower their center of gravity while their long necks arch and stretch forward and down at the same time as their heads angle back upward in the direction of the udder, and then their lips reach even farther and finally make the connection.

My guest, the friend of a friend, had come out to Proud Spirit for a tour of our operation. We were standing together watching mother and baby when she inquired about my plans for weaning. I was grinning proudly over how wonderfully adorable our little Riley was, as though I were personally responsible for her downy soft coat, butterfly eyelashes, and fuzzy mane that had a mind of its own.

*Gentle Ranger
and Melanie
sharing a
moment*

But there was that darn question again. The beaming smile on my face slowly drained away.

I couldn't believe how many times someone had asked me that since Jesse gave birth to Riley only three months before. One person even asked me when I was going to wean her when Riley was not yet two weeks old. I wondered why this was such a major topic of conversation. I never even thought about it until someone else brought it up. I apparently had a glaring inability to grasp the importance of deciding when one plans to wean a foal, and this failing of mine seemed to vex the entire equestrian community.

"I'm not," I said and put my hands firmly on my hips in a show of conviction.

My guest chuckled, as though I were kidding and cocked her head to the side. "What do you mean 'you're not'?" she asked.

"I'm not, that's all," I said and shrugged my shoulders. "I'm not going to wean her."

"But you have to wean her. She'll bring the mare down." My guest was referring to the possibility of a mare losing weight when a foal is allowed to nurse too long. But that might only happen if the mare had been "bred back" and was once again in foal. When it happens in the wild, natural instincts kick in and the mare, completely of her own accord, will no longer let a foal nurse. The same thing would happen if a domestic mare was bred right away. I wondered to myself why we think we must always interfere. Regardless, it was a moot point as Jesse would never be bred again. Riley could nurse until the cows came home as far as I was concerned.

"This mare isn't going to be bred again," I told my guest. "The foal won't bring her down."

"But how in the world are you going to train her if she isn't weaned? You have to wean her," she insisted.

"That's hogwash," I said. "She'll come to understand the halter, and being led, and having her feet trimmed, and everything else she needs to know. All while she still has access to her mom. There's simply no reason to wean her. It'll happen naturally."

My guest nodded, albeit suspiciously, and finally gave up. "Huh," she said. "I never heard of such a thing."

It was fall of 2004. Jim and I had been rescuing horses in need for over twelve years and were caring for nearly forty at that time. In all those years, and all the horses we had taken in, most of them were older, even elderly. There had been several that were under ten and a few that were even under five. But we'd never had a baby until Riley. Furthermore, we did no breeding, as that would make us part of the problem, so the odds were against our ever having another one.

Riley was a delightful gift. She enriched our lives in every aspect and Jim was thoroughly smitten with her. We both were, and both of us were finding it difficult to get our daily chores complete because we spent so much time playing with her and fussing over her. We felt blessed to have her and were abundantly confident that she would be a once-in-a-lifetime experience for us.

I have since learned, however, that there are ramifications in life for thinking that something will never happen. In all ways, it pretty much assures that the something you thought would never happen actually will. Just a few shorts weeks after Riley turned three months old, our sanctuary and our lives would be sweetly rich with babies.

One afternoon I received a call from a friend's daughter. Her name was Amy, and she was a lovely young lady in her early twenties. Amy was a genuine horse lover. She had been around them her entire life and was a skilled rider. She already had a successful business as a riding instructor. The day Amy phoned me she sounded upset. One of her clients, a couple named Randal, had a twelve-year-old daughter who was one of Amy's pupils.

"Two weekends ago I showed up for our scheduled lesson and no one was home," Amy told me. "I didn't think too much about it. I just figured they forgot—things happen. But the same thing happened last weekend. So I tried calling them for several days in a row. No one has ever been home and I left a bunch of messages."

"Could they be on vacation?" I asked.

"No," Amy said. "They would have told me. And they would have hired me to take care of the horses. They always have in the past. Something strange was going on. I've since found out what. And that's why I'm calling you."

I waited for her to go on.

"When I could never reach anyone, I started to worry about the horses. I mean, I was worried about the Randals too, but horses can't take care of themselves. They're all out on pasture and they have a pond for drinking, so they have food and water. But I knew something had to be wrong and the horses couldn't go unattended like this forever. I started driving out there every day to check on them. Well, today the place was swarming with local deputies and FBI agents."

"FBI! What in the world happened?"

"Well, I'm still in shock. The Randals took their two kids to his mother's house and fled the country. They're both being brought up on charges of embezzling millions, along with real estate fraud and all sorts of things."

"Geez, I guess you never really know someone, do you?"

"That's the truth. The deputies asked me all sorts of questions. I told them who I was and that I was employed by the Randals in the past to care for the horses. And I also said that I was very worried about what would happen to them now. One of the deputies had some short little discussion with the FBI guys. Then they told me they had bigger fish to fry than what to do with five horses. They asked me if I would remove them from the property and said I could do whatever I felt was right."

"So what are you going to do?" I asked

"Well, they're all really gorgeous Paints. I know I can find good homes for three of them. But there's an older gelding and a yearling colt. I was wondering if you could take both of them."

"You don't think you can find them homes?"

"I could, but I'd feel better about them coming to you. The older guy would be fine for riding, but I've sorta got a soft spot in my heart for him. He hasn't had the best life. He deserves what you can give him at Proud Spirit."

I smiled over Amy's kindness toward animals. "Okay," I said. I also trusted her instincts. If she felt the gelding deserved to simply come be a horse at Proud Spirit, I believed her. "But what about the colt?" I asked. "Is there a reason he couldn't be adopted?"

There was a pause on the other end of the phone. "Oh, Melanie, I know it might seem silly, but he's really bonded to the gelding and I can't stand the thought of separating them. He's just a baby."

"It's not silly, Amy." I smiled. "Go ahead and bring them both out."

Amy arrived the next day with the two Paint horses. We put them in a paddock together until we could get the colt gelded, then they would go out with the herd. We named the young horse Jackson and the older gelding became Ranger.

I do not question why a horse finds his way to our sanctuary. The reasons are usually clear, and most are here as a result of abuse, neglect, or injury. Some are simply old and no one else wants them. But every once in a while a horse comes to us whom others would say "doesn't really need to be here." Ranger and Jackson could easily have fallen into that category. There was nothing "wrong" with them, someone might say. They should be adopted out so someone could be using them. But that's not how we operate. I don't believe a horse must be in service to man to be useful. And I don't analyze or dissect how or why a horse finds his way to us. Perhaps Ranger and Jackson didn't really need us, but shortly after they arrived Ranger would demonstrate, on a very profound level, how much we needed him. A little later on he would help me heal a broken heart.

Remarkably, we now had two babies. But another one was on the way. Just days after Ranger and Jackson arrived we brought home a young filly. She belonged to a woman who was going through a difficult time in her life, requiring her to part with her four horses. She found homes for three of them, but the fourth one had a slight problem with her legs and she would never be able to bear the weight of a rider. No one wanted her. We named her Cocoa. She was just four months old.

That gave us three horses under one year of age: Riley, Jackson, and Cocoa.

Then Tuxedo arrived. He was a young Standardbred off the track. He had injured a tendon as a baby and spent the next few months of his young life locked in a stall. His trainer was going to put him down after it became clear he would never recover enough to run in competition. He was just taking up space. The colt's owner was contacted. Thankfully, this person had a conscience and hated the thought of him being put down when he could actually live a very nice life. He, in turn, found us and we agreed to allow the horse to come to Proud Spirit and live out his life. They brought him to us the very same week Cocoa arrived. He was the same age as Jackson and the two young colts became good buddies.

It was during this time that I recalled reading an article that had appeared in a major equestrian magazine. I was interested because it was entitled "Help Your Foal Grow." We now had four babies and I wanted to learn all I could. The article highlighted a grant that had been awarded to a group of individuals who were studying the marked difference in the health and growth of two groups of newborn foals. One group was allowed time out of their stalls to run and frolic. The second group was kept confined to their stalls and never let out. After reading the article I remember feeling nearly dumbfounded that someone actually felt this needed studying. And that they were actually paid. I also found it hard to believe that a reputable equestrian magazine actually ran the article.

Who wouldn't know that *all* living creatures need to move around, use their muscles, and run and romp to be healthy and grow? The concluding sentence in the article said something like, "So whenever possible, allow your foals time to stretch their legs." To me, it was asinine. If it weren't so sad that this major publication thought its readers needed to be told something so fundamentally obvious, it would have been laughable. It was even sadder that there were people out there, breeding and raising foals, who actually kept them confined.

Tuxedo provided a perfect example of this grant-funded study. We named him Tuxedo because when he arrived his gleaming coat was pure black and he had three brilliant white socks from never spending any time outside of his stall, making him look as though he were wearing a tuxedo. This would change soon enough once he was allowed to live as he should. His coat would eventually fade in the sun and his white socks would be caked with mud from playing in the creek.

Because of the way he had previously lived, Tuxedo's muscles were underdeveloped and he was small for his age. When he arrived at Proud Spirit he had no self-confidence and everything scared him. A natural environment was completely foreign to him. He snorted at bushes and fallen tree limbs. He was terrified of the large storks that roosted in our pond. Even a leaf blowing across the pasture was cause for concern. It's a terrible disservice to never expose horses to the world around them.

At the opposite end of the spectrum stood our little Riley. She'd never been stalled for any period and had spent every day of her young life exploring the thirty-acre pasture, interacting with, and learning from, an entire herd of horses. She was fit and muscled, and absolutely fearless about her natural environment.

A few weeks after Tuxedo arrived I received an e-mail from a friend who runs a horse rescue organization in New Hampshire called Live and Let Live Farm. Teresa Paradis is a kindred spirit and our philosophies about horses mirror one another. She was deeply involved in the Premarin issue (or PMU—Pregnant Mare Urine) and was an integral link in rescuing hundreds of slaughter-bound foals. Teresa was going to be receiving an entire semi-load of three-month-old foals, 150 of them, from a Premarin farm in Canada. But the owner would not release the babies unless they were all pre-adopted by private individuals instead of being placed in the hands of a rescue organization. With all of the recent media attention on Premarin farms, it would look better for the owners if the foals were "adopted" rather than "rescued."

My friend Teresa wrote to tell me that she had every single baby pre-adopted, except for two of them. She wanted to know if I would help her network and try to get the funds for the release of the two remaining foals. Time was running out. Jim and I looked at the photos Teresa had attached in her email. It was heartbreaking to see these three-month-old foals crammed together in the holding pens. They looked terrified and lost. We agreed to come up with the funds to adopt one of them as private individuals, not as Proud Spirit. The adoption fee, hauling expenses, and medical papers would be one thousand dollars.

I immediately put out an e-mail of my own to a list of friends on behalf of the final remaining foal. I explained the entire situation and told everyone that Jim and I were taking one and asked if there was anyone who could take the second one. I attached a picture of the lone baby in my e-mail. That very evening my phone rang.

"Mel," the voice said when I picked up. "If you have room for the second foal at Proud Spirit, Sue and I will pay her adoption fee."

"Jean!" I hollered. "You will? Oh, this is wonderful!"

Jean was a fairly new friend in my life, but had become as dear to me as if I'd known her for years and years. She lived in North Carolina and we'd become acquainted after she read my book and had contacted me to talk about our shared love of horses. Her daughter, Sue, lived an hour north of our Florida ranch. We were able to meet the previous year when Jean was visiting Sue, and we had since become great friends.

"Do you think you might have room for both of them?" she asked.

"Yes, absolutely. We'll work it out. This really is wonderful of you," I repeated.

"Sue's even picked out a name already," Jean said.

"She has?" I laughed. "Did you send her the filly's picture?"

"Yes, she saw it. Sue thinks her markings look like clouds and she thought of the name Nimbus."

My end of the telephone line went silent.

"Mel," Jean said, "are you there?"

After a few more uncomfortable moments I managed a cough.

"Mel?" Jean said.

"Eh hem," I finally sputtered. "Nimbus, huh? Well, isn't that . . . um, well. Hmmm. How interesting. Nimbus. Sort of like cumulous, but in a different pattern."

"You don't like it?" Jean asked.

"No, no, no," I shot out. "It's a great name . . . for a cloud."

"You don't like it," Jean stated, her voice tinged with disappointment.

"How about you and Sue call her Nimbus, um, amongst yourselves. You know, just for now. Till they arrive. And then we can talk more it about later. And maybe, you know, maybe I'll call her something else after I get to know her," I told Jean, trying to sound cheerful and diplomatic. "Definitely something else," I mumbled to myself.

Our two little PMU foals arrived one month later. I decided to name the foal that Jim and I adopted Dixie. And the other little foal, the one who had almost been left behind until Jean and Sue intervened, was named Ruby. Jean and Sue have since concurred that Ruby is a perfect name for the little filly. Up until then the two babies had only been a number. We felt some good ol' Southern names would help with their new beginning.

Now we had six babies under one year old. It was amazing. I never would have believed this would happen and we loved every hour we spent with them. Jim and I were thrilled that all these youngsters were with us. We were truly happy that we could give them the life they deserved, even though there were moments that continued to remind us of their sad beginnings.

Except for Riley, they all seemed a little lost. They had poor social skills as a result of being taken from their dams so young and being isolated from other horses. They hadn't been allowed to function in a herd or live a normal life. We turned them out with our main herd on thirty acres, but most of the adults would run them off. Not viciously, just keeping them at a distance. The babies eventually banded together and formed their own small group. But they didn't seem settled.

Then we noticed something extraordinary beginning to happen. Day after day we watched as Ranger, the big Paint gelding, separated himself from the other adults. We would see him standing off in the distance, happily grazing on his own. If another adult came over to him, he moved away. Slowly, one by one, all the babies gravitated to Ranger and he did not run them off or move away. Finally they were all clustered around him. It was astonishing. He was taking them under his wing.

Ranger and the babies had formed a sub-herd of seven and suddenly they never left his side. Ranger was a tall horse with beautiful markings. Day after day we saw him surrounded by these little waifs, his regal and stately head sticking up out of the fray. Ranger was always gentle and kind to the babies, but he backed up the equine rules with a nip to the shoulder or a hoof to the rump. After several weeks we finally saw the sullen youngsters come alive. They were running and playing. They were getting stronger and gaining confidence. Ranger had helped them become balanced and secure.

Over the next few years we would witness numerous events just as miraculous as this one, where Ranger became a guardian or helped one of his herdmates heal.

When a visitor points at the big Paint gelding and wants to know his name and why he is here, I smile and tell them, "That's Ranger. And he's here because *we* need *him*."

Author note: Premarin farms are facilities that collect the urine of an estimated forty thousand mares who are repeatedly bred and kept in horrible living conditions. Their urine is used to produce female hormone replacement therapy (HRT) drugs. The forty thousand foals they give birth to every year are considered just a "byproduct" of this industry and are sent to slaughter by the thousands. Organizations such as Live and Let Live Farm (www.liveandletlivefarm.org) and United Pegasus (www.united pegasus.com) are deeply committed to this disturbing issue. The broad implications are extremely controversial and would require an entire chapter to explore. I would encourage everyone to look into, at the very least, how these groups are involved and see what you can do to help.

The Move

I STOOD LOOKING AT THE NEAT ROWS OF HALTERS that my friend Carla and I had laid out on the concrete pad of our driveway. She had just helped me drag a large Tupperware tub from the tack room of our barn out to the yard. The tub was filled with the sixty or seventy halters that we had collected over the years. Carla and I sorted through them all to find the ones that were in the best shape. We were preparing to put them on the horses.

The vet checks had been completed, the paperwork was in order, and all the horses had been brought in from the pastures and were calmly grazing in the central paddock near the barn of our Florida ranch. They were ready for the three fifty-three-foot semitrailers that were on their way from Ocala and expected any moment. The horses were blissfully unaware of the monumental task that was about to unfold. They didn't know that they were about to embark on a journey that would take them halfway across the country and forever change Proud Spirit Horse Sanctuary. The day had arrived for us to move our horses to the

Getting ready to leave the ranch in Florida for the new facility in Arkansas

new ranch in Arkansas.

I nervously counted the halters one more time, making sure that we had the right number set out. Eight rows with five in each row. Forty halters. The astonishing realization hit me. *We were moving forty horses.*

In addition to Carla, there were about ten other friends at the house that day. Jim and three of our nine dogs had already left for Arkansas the week before. One of us had to go on ahead to receive the horses and one of us had to stay behind to get them on the road. We decided that Jim would be the one to prepare for their arrival at our new ranch. I was alone at the ranch in Florida and several close friends had come out to help the day the horses were leaving. Some were equestrians whom I had asked to assist with loading them onto the trailers. One friend had come to film the event with her video camera. Another was taking pictures.

Others had driven out to our ranch simply because they wanted to watch, and others had come to say goodbye. They had all parked their cars and trucks up in our yard to stay out of the way of the expected semis.

Carla came to stand beside me. She put her arm around my shoulder and gave me a squeeze. "You okay?" she asked when she saw my face.

I must have looked like a deer in the headlights. I took a deep breath and looked up at her without answering. I saw that her deep green eyes glimmered with unshed tears. She pulled me to her in a hug. We had been close neighbors and good friends for eight years. We saw each other practically every single day, if not to actually speak, then at least to wave at each other across our adjoining pastures. We could see each other's barns and keep an eye on each other's horses. I relied on her for so much and it would be heartbreaking to say goodbye to her. I smiled at her and finally nodded weakly in response to her question.

Suddenly, I heard another friend, who was standing behind us, sharply inhale. "Oh my God," she said quietly. And then she shouted, "They're here. The trucks are here!"

Carla quickly patted my back and left me. I was vaguely aware of her scooping up an armful of halters and heading out to where the horses stood. But I didn't move or turn around. I felt immobilized. An enormous part of my life was ending. At the same time, the culmination of all of my dreams for these horses was coming true. I shut my eyes and slowly inhaled, filling my lungs till it hurt. And then I slowly let the air back out. My emotions were ragged.

As I joined my friends to watch the trucks pull in, I played pat-a-cake with my own hands in an attempt to dry my sweating palms and disperse the pent-up nervous energy that was beating in my chest.

Three enormous horse trailers, their aluminum sides gleaming in the sun, rumbled into our ranch and stacked themselves along the driveway.

I introduced myself to the lead driver. His name was John; he in turn introduced me to the entire crew. There were three people per truck, two to share the driving and one to ride in the back with the horses.

It was the first time I had actually seen the inside of a fifty-three-foot semitrailer designed for horses, and it truly was amazing. The trailers were outfitted with removable panels, walls, and gates to create stalls and aisleways. The manager of the shipping company had sent me a configuration of the proposed floor plan several weeks before. I was allowed to pair all the horses with their closest herdmate in an appropriate sized stall. Their names had already been penciled into the little diagram he had sent. In the mix we had miniatures and draft horses, a dam and her nursing foal, and a few horses who needed to be stalled alone because they didn't play nice. All of the positions had already been assigned and all the coordinating paperwork and health certificates of each horse, in each trailer, and in each particular stall, was on the clipboard I now clutched to my chest.

Huge ramps were dropped down from the bellies of the semis and then covered in thick sisal carpeting to prevent the horses from slipping. We were ready to begin loading the horses. I stood in the middle of the paddock while my friends grabbed the remaining halters from the driveway.

I started calling out directions. "Char, will you bring Phoenix? He goes in the same stall with Dually." Char nodded and went to walk the elderly grey Thoroughbred to the trailer. "Chris," I called out, pointing at our smallest Miniature horse, Wrangler. "The minis go in the very back stalls, so they need to be loaded first." Chris and Char are husband and wife, and two of our closest friends. Chris is a big, tall man with soft blue eyes and an engaging smile. He went to halter Wrangler, making the little horse appear even smaller. "No, no," I called out to someone else, "Rosie and Cracker ride together. They go in this trailer." The activity swirled around me for nearly two hours.

Finally, all the horses were loaded. I stepped up into each one of the trailers to double check on everyone and make sure they were settled. I touched each one as I walked along and whispered calming words. I came to the very back of the trailer with the stall holding the four minis: Wrangler, Rodeo, Misty, and Scout.

"Aw, you poor kids can't see over your wall," I said to them. John was standing directly behind me securing a latch on one of the panels.

"What's wrong?" he asked.

"Oh, nothing. I was just talking to them about their wall being so high. They can't see over the top, but they'll be fine."

"Well, we can fix that." John cheerfully turned on his heel and trotted down the ramp of the trailer. "Hey, Bill," I heard him call. "Will you help me a second?"

There was some shuffling around in one of the outside compartments of the semi. John and Bill returned to the aisleway where I stood, each of them carrying several aluminum panels.

"You hold onto those guys for just a second," he said to me, nodding at the minis. I put my arms out to keep the little horses where they were. John and Bill quickly removed the higher partition and replaced it with several lower ones.

"There ya go," John smiled.

Now the minis could look over the top of their wall and see their herdmates.

"You are a good man." I smiled happily as I patted John's back. "Thank you."

I handed John the three manila envelopes containing all the horse's health certificates and transportation documents. He took them from me and shuffled through the numerous sheets of paper, making sure he had everything he needed. Satisfied, he returned everything to its proper envelope, pushed the brass clasps back in place, and then looked over at me.

"You know, I have to tell you something," he said. "When we pulled up here and saw all those horses in that paddock there, I looked over at my driver and said, 'I hope you know we're gonna be here all day gettin' this herd loaded.' I figured it was gonna be a nightmare 'cause they're all rescue horses. But I gotta tell ya, I've been around horses for over forty years, and I been hauling professionally for at least twenty. I've transported top show horses and Olympic contenders. I want you to know that I have never been around such calm, well-behaved, and level-minded horses as these were today."

Several of the other drivers were standing nearby. All of them nodded and expressed similar sentiments. I smiled proudly and thanked everyone while they continued to comment about how remarkable it was that not one single horse was difficult to load. Everyone one of them just walked right onto the ramp and up into the trailer.

I knew it was a testament to the way our horses are treated. They trust.

"Well," John said as he glanced around, "I guess we're ready to go."

It hit me—my horses were leaving. The emotion washed over me. I nodded at John, but didn't trust myself to speak. My vision blurred with tears.

"Are you gonna be okay?" he asked with a gentle smile.

I could only let out a small laugh. I nodded once again. We stared at each other. He had been incredibly kind and patient with the horses and extremely kind to me. All of the drivers had been. I had already thanked each of them extensively, and they were now back at their own trucks getting ready to go. Except John.

My eyes bored into his as I struggled to find the words to thank him once again and tell him one final thing. He was not made uncomfortable by my scrutiny and looked directly back into my eyes with an easy, confident smile. He could see how emotional I was and he reached out to put his hand on my shoulder. He gave me a brotherly, teasing shake to ease some of the tension.

"We're gonna take good care of 'em," he said, squeezing my shoulder. "Okay?"

I nodded again and lifted my hand in the direction of the trailers without taking my eyes from his. "These are my babies," I whispered over the lump in my throat. "These horses are everything to me. They are my life."

He smiled at me and nodded. "Then let's get them to their new home," he said.

My friends surrounded me as the three semitrailers headed down our long driveway. We watched until they rounded the bend in the county road a half-mile from our house and we could no longer see them. I tearfully hugged the friends who had to leave. I would be making my departure for Arkansas the following day, so we said our goodbyes. The friends who remained helped me clean out the barn and a few other tasks. And then there were more hugs and tears, and they too were gone. Except for our six dogs who would be riding with me to the new ranch, I was completely alone.

I went into the house to go over the list of things I needed to do before I could get on the road the next day. Our house was essentially empty, but I looked around at the few items that still needed to be packed and boxes that still needed to be stowed in my truck. After all the chaos and stress of the day, it seemed I had quite a bit of work to do. While I sat at the island in the kitchen going over my list, my stomach growled, reminding me that I hadn't eaten anything. I went to the fridge and leaned against the counter while I ate a cup of yogurt and allowed myself a few minutes to relax and calm down.

I tossed the empty yogurt container into the trash and looked around the house once again. I recalled something I needed from my truck. With a sigh, I walked back outside. I was preoccupied with my list of everything that needed to be done, but for some reason I was keenly aware of the sound of my footsteps as I quickly tapped along the concrete and made my way to the pickup. I reached for the door handle but didn't lift the latch.

All of a sudden, the silence of our ranch enveloped me like a wave. I let my hand slip from the door handle and fall back to my side as I turned in the direction of the pastures. I almost felt like I was in shock. My remaining chores were forgotten as I moved away from the house and walked slowly to the nearest fence line.

We had lived with thirty-plus horses for nearly twelve years. Now our property stood empty. It was unbearably empty. Even the air smelled different. The horses had only been gone a few hours, but already the air was no longer familiar to me; it didn't smell as sweet. And I couldn't believe the silence. There were no swishing tails, no shuffling feet, nor the delicate sound of them munching on grass. No whinnies, no knickers, and no horses clearing their noses. I was literally overwhelmed by the silence.

To me, it is always very meaningful in life when you know something in your head, but then something happens to make you realize it in your heart. At that moment I knew, I absolutely knew in my heart, that I could never live without horses.

I crawled through the fence and walked out into the pasture. I slowly pivoted around in a circle and took in the empty pastures with a heavy heart. I thought about all the horses who had come to us since the beginning of this sanctuary. I thought about the forty horses who, right this very minute, were on their way to the new ranch. I recalled the ones who would not be making the journey. My eyes rested on the place where they were buried. My mischievous Dusty, poor little Annie, gentle Marshal, sweet Hank, gallant Dancer and his beloved Maddy, Bravo, Max, JJ, Sunny, Mighty, the little baby colt . . . and so many, many others.

My precious Cody.

I walked over to the raw patch of dirt where she had been buried just weeks before. I kneeled down beside her grave and silently wept that she did not live to see the dream of this move come true, this dream which she had started. I reached out and smoothed the dirt with my open hand as though I were actually touching her. She had been failing in the months preceding our move.

I recalled the day when I knew she would not be able to make the twenty-four-hour trailer ride or handle the stress of moving. Shortly thereafter I had our vet come out to humanely euthanize Cody. It tore at my heart like a knife, but I knew it was the right thing to do. I laid her purple halter at her side that day after she was gone and put a copy of *The Horses of Proud Spirit* under her cheek to be buried with her. Hers is the first chapter. The entire book, and every reason this sanctuary exists, is because of her.

Now, I lifted a handful of the fresh dirt that covered her grave then let it sift through my fingers and fall back to the earth. This life we are given is so fragile, so fleeting. I pondered how anyone could have looked into her liquid brown eyes and been unkind to her. I wondered why anyone would waste the precious few days they have on this earth abusing an animal. But I silently thanked whatever power stands above us all for bringing Cody to me. I missed her desperately and put my hand over my heart and tapped my chest. "You are with me, beautiful girl," I told her through my tears. "You'll always be with me."

I turned away and went back into the house to call Jim at the new ranch. I was still choked with tears.

"Jim," I cried out as soon as he picked up.

"What's wrong?" he asked.

"They're on the way," I said, still crying.

"What's wrong?" he repeated.

"Nothing's wrong," I cried.

"Everything's okay?"

"Yes."

"Why are you crying?" he breathed out.

Men, I thought. "Because," I wailed. "Because they're gone, they're on the way. It's all coming true. This dream is coming true. And because Cody's *not* coming. I miss her so much. And . . . and because it's so quiet here. And—" I stopped to get my breath. I was beginning to feel a little hysterical and started crying harder. "And because it's so *God-awful* quiet here," I told him again through my tears. "It's horrible!"

"Okay, listen," he said. "Calm down. Don't think about the old ranch being empty. Think about the new one being full. Think about what they're coming to. Okay?"

I couldn't talk.

"Okay?" Jim said more earnestly.

"Okay," I managed, but it sounded more like a pathetic squeak coming through my constricted throat.

"I'll call you the second the trucks pull in," he said. "Okay?"

I squeaked once again in response.

"And then you'll be here in no time . . . okay?"

Squeak.

The Arrival

THE HORSES HAD LEFT TWENTY-FOUR HOURS AGO. I was still at the old ranch in Florida. I had several delays and was unable to get on the road as planned. Finally, everything was taken care of. My cell phone rang just as I was ready to go.

"They're here!" It was Jim. "All three trailers are here."

I felt an oppressive cloud of stress lift away. "Is everybody all right?" I asked.

"I don't know. They're just pulling in the driveway," he said. "I haven't even spoken to any of the drivers yet. I'm standing out here directing them where to go."

I could hear the rumble of the diesel engines through Jim's cell phone. "I'll call you back in a little bit, okay?" he said.

"No!" I yelled. "Don't hang up. I want to hear what's going on."

I couldn't believe I was missing seeing this. When Jim and I were discussing who would leave Florida first so one of us would be at the new ranch to receive the horses, and who would leave

The horses of Proud Spirit exploring their new home

second to make sure they were safely on the road, we decided it would be better if he went first, and I stayed behind. Now I was regretting the decision.

I wanted to witness our beautiful horses getting off that trailer. I wanted to see their reaction to stepping out to the pastures of their new home for the first time. These were horses who had been abused, starved, and neglected before they came to us. Some had been unwanted and abandoned, while others had been cruelly confined to dark stalls for years at a time, unable to move or interact with other horses. In just moments they would be running free as a herd on 320 acres of rolling hills, living the life every horse should live. The life they deserved.

"Honey," Jim laughed. "I can't stand here talking to you on the phone. I need to help these guys unload the horses."

"No!" I yelled again. "Can't you just leave your phone on and put it in your pocket or something so I can hear everything?"

"Mel," Jim pleaded.

"Don't hang up! I'm begging you—"

There were some shuffling noises. "Yeah, you're fine right there," I heard Jim call over the diesel engines. His voice sounded distant as if he had moved the phone away from his mouth. I could hear truck doors slamming and muffled conversation. "The other two trucks can stay right where they are," he added.

"What's happening?" I yelled.

"That gate," Jim said. I could hear someone talking in the background, but I couldn't hear what he was saying, and then both Jim and whoever it was were laughing.

"Who was that?" I hollered.

"No," Jim said, his voice still in the distance. "Everyone is being turned right out to this main pasture."

"What's happening!"

"Yeah, we'll take them through that gate," Jim said.

"How are the horses?" I screamed. There were more indiscernible noises and more laughter.

"Tell me about it," Jim laughed.

"What's going on, dammit!"

"How'd they all do?" I heard Jim say. There was a muffled answer.

"What'd he say—" I yelled. Oh crap, I muttered to myself in frustration as I jumped up and down. "What'd he say!"

Suddenly the phone was being shuffled around, and then Jim's voice was right next to my ear. "Mel," he said.

"Oh good, you're back," I puffed. "What'd he say? What'd he say? Lemme talk to John."

"Mel—"

"He's the lead driver. Put 'im on. Put John on."

"Mel! I'm gonna hang up. You're driving me nuts."

"No! Jim! Jim, don't you dare hang up this phone," I yelled. "Dammit to hell," I said into dead air space.

A half-hour later my phone rang again. It was Jim. "They're

all unloaded. And they're all fine," he said. I could hear the smile in his voice.

"What are they doing? Tell me what they're doing."

"They're . . . they're just grazing," he said.

"No, no, no," I said. "Tell me what they're doing."

"Honey, they're just grazing."

"No, go out there with the phone and tell me what they're doing. I want to know what each one of them is doing."

"Each one of them? All forty horses?"

"Yes, I want to know what each one of them is doing." I was crying with joy and laughing through my tears. "Tell me exactly what they're doing."

"Okay," he said. I could hear the clang of a chain as Jim opened a gate. "Let's see. Strut is relaxing with his left rear leg cocked, just a little. Oops, now it's his right one and he's decided to graze. Wrangler and Scout are running around like little madmen. Rodeo is pooping. Pie just pinned her ears at Misty. Tango is pooping. Normy is looking over at the lake as though he's never seen anything quite like it. Riley is trying to nurse, but Jesse keeps walking away. Ruby is pooping. Tuxedo and Jackson are playing and nipping each other's manes. Charlie is rolling. Rosie and Cracker have already wandered off by themselves. Biscuit is . . ."

I listened to Jim for the next twenty minutes as he told me what each horse was doing while the tears streamed down my face. I could not have been any happier. And for standing out in the pasture surrounded by forty horses as he painted a detailed description of the lovely scene, I silently took back all the mean and hateful things I called him for hanging up on me.

Two days later I pulled into the driveway of our new home in Arkansas. Before I looked around the yard or even walked into the house, I ran to the nearest gate and went to find the horses. We have a total of 320 acres—160 acres of lush rolling pasture dotted with oaks, elms, maples, pines, redbuds, and dogwoods, all surrounded by 160 acres of dense woods. Right in the middle of it all there is a sparkling fourteen-acre spring-fed lake where the horses can swim and cool off.

I saw the herd off in the distance. I headed in their direction and broke into a run, anxious to touch each and every one. As I drew close I reveled at the very sight of them. "Hi guys!" I called out. I stood among them and breathed deep of their smell. There is nothing that compares to the sweet, earthy smell of horses. And I soaked up the sound of them simply being horses.

I thought of Cody. I let my gaze drift over the hills of our new home. "You're here, aren't you, girl?" I whispered. "You're here. I can feel you."

When I finally returned to the house, Jim reached out for me. I went to move into his arms, but he grabbed my shoulder and turned me around.

"What are you doing?" I asked. I felt him lift my hair off the nape of my neck. When I turned back to him I saw he had something pinched between his thumb and forefinger. It was a tick.

"Welcome to Arkansas," he smirked.

A Visitor

I WAS STANDING AT THE WINDOW OF A BACK BEDROOM in our new home. We had been here for only a few short weeks, but I was still mesmerized by the view of our horses grazing on all this incredible land. I imagined I would be mesmerized by it for the rest of my life. My hands were resting on the window sill and I was absent mindedly running my fingernails over the grooves in the wood. They had been left there by the dogs of our home's previous owner, Marilee Pratt.

I recalled that there had been a twin bed under this window when Marilee had lived here. Her beloved dogs used to jump up and use the sill as a perch for watching the world go by. Their nails had scratched the soft wood. Jim and I intended to do some updating to the house. We planned to tile the floors, freshen up the paint, and get new appliances; we would make this home our own. But it struck me that I would not sand the marks out of this window sill. It was part of the life that made the home what it was to Marilee and what, I had no doubt, it would become to us.

Granny

Over the next several months I would discover many things in and around our new house that would remind me of Marilee, and I would leave these little reminders just the way I found them.

Marilee and her husband retired in the early '70s. They were both career military personnel and had moved to Mena to raise cattle and horses and to enjoy everything this little town had to offer. Marilee's husband was a formidable man. Everyone continued to refer to him as the Colonel, even after he was retired. But it was Marilee who became such an enormous presence in the community and made an everlasting impression on anyone who met her.

She was actively involved with the local Humane Society and devoted her life to making the lives of homeless animals better. She also supported a spay and neuter program to help curb over-population of unwanted cats and dogs. And with a generous heart, she opened her own home as a safe haven for numerous strays.

I remembered the day Jim and I came to look at this house. Marilee had been a widow for several years by that time and taking care of the ranch on her own was getting to be too much. She made the heartbreaking decision to sell her home of thirty years and return to her hometown in Illinois to be closer to family. She met us out in the driveway the day we arrived with Sandy, our realtor. Sandy made the introductions and then asked if we would like to begin by seeing the house. But we were more interested in the land. Before going inside, I asked if Jim and I could walk around a little on our own. We couldn't really tell what the property looked like from where we stood and I wanted to get a feel for the place. The land had to be perfect. This move was for our horses.

Jim and I left Sandy and Marilee out front and continued walking along the driveway, in the direction of the barn. We came up to the fence line and had a perfect view of the pastures—160 acres of beautiful rolling hills all surrounded by dense woods creating a cocoon of privacy and peace. The shimmering lake, situated in the middle of the pastures, was rimmed with dogwood and redbud trees and made the perfect backdrop for the Ouachita mountain range in the distance. I can't speak for Jim, but it took my breath away. We looked at each other and neither one of us said a word. We knew that we had found the perfect home for our horses.

Jim and I walked back to where Sandy and Marilee were talking in the driveway. I smiled and said, "You can take us back to the office. We want to make an offer." Sandy was slightly flummoxed. "You haven't seen inside," she said, pointing at the house.

"That's okay," I said. "This land is everything we've dreamed about."

"But we have four more ranches to see," she added.

"You can cancel the appointments," I said. We all started laughing. I turned to Marilee and said, "You have a beautiful place here. I hope this works out."

She nodded and I could see tears gathering in her eyes. "I just want to see horses here again," she told me. I immediately looked at Sandy and smiled.

"Did you tell her—" I began. Earlier, when we were back at

Sandy's office, we had told her all about Proud Spirit and our horses as we described the type of property we were looking for.

"No, I never said a word," she said. And then she looked at Marilee. "Jim and Melanie are the founders of a horse sanctuary, Mrs. Pratt. They'll be relocating from Florida and bringing forty rescued horses with them when they move."

Marilee turned to look at me, but we did not speak. We simply smiled at each other in quiet understanding.

Jim was talking to Sandy, asking various questions about the property. Marilee and I went into the house and she showed me around each room as we talked. After a few moments of chatting, she and I developed a lasting bond. We learned that we had a lot in common, primarily that we were both passionate about animals.

Jim and I went back to Sandy's office and submitted an offer, and the transaction did work out. Marilee and I have stayed in touch to this very day. I frequently send her pictures of the horses getting a drink from the lake, which I still refer to as "Marilee's Lake," and of them grazing on the beautiful rolling pastures that she and the Colonel cleared back in the '70s.

• • •

I turned away from the window where I had been standing and looked down at the stack of boxes I was supposed to be unpacking. It was a task that I was actually enjoying. For each empty box that I flung out to the driveway emphasized the fact that we were really here. But I was discovering, more and more, that it was difficult to get any work done. I couldn't stop staring out the windows and I was spending too much time marveling at the view and watching our horses grazing on the lush hills.

With a contented sigh, I kneeled down on the floor and pulled one of the boxes over to my side. I took out my pocket knife and cut the packing tape. Suddenly my dogs started barking. It was not a playful bark that happens when two of them are romping together. All of them were barking. They were in alert mode which meant that we had a visitor. I had no idea who it might be.

We really hadn't had a chance to meet many people yet. There were only a few other houses on our road. We had met our neighbors, and had already become friends, but I knew they were at work. And we were so far out in the country I couldn't imagine who would just be stopping in without calling first. I could hear the dogs scrambling through the kitchen and then on into the living room. They were vying for the best position at the front windows to bark at whoever must be here.

I hurried out to the living room to see who it might be and to quiet the dogs. Nine of them barking at a fevered pitch could be fairly annoying. "Hey!" I hollered over the din as I looked out the window. I saw that a pickup truck I did not recognize was coming down the driveway, moving very slowly. The dogs ignored my effort to quiet them. I tried again. "Shhh!" I said, just exactly the way Cesar Millan, the Dog Whisperer, says it. They continued barking. I made a mental note that I needed to do something, someday, about my unbalanced pack. Oh, the noise they were making! In another attempt to channel the Dog Whisperer I employed another one of his techniques as I scooted along the line of all nine dogs. "SHHH, SHHH, SHHH—" I puffed at each one, in conjunction with that quick stiff-fingered jab to the throat he uses to get their attention. I started to feel a little dizzy by the time I got to the ninth dog, sorta like that feeling you get from blowing up a balloon too fast. A few of the dogs glanced up at me briefly in a fleeting moment of irritation, but the barking continued.

I took another look out the window and saw that whoever was coming down our driveway was also pulling a trailer. "That's enough!" I yelled at the dogs. Well, it might have been more like a scream. Like a banshee scream. But it worked. Simultaneously their ears, which had all been pricked in attention, fell dejectedly flat back on their heads as they reluctantly moved away from the window. "Sorry, Mr. Millan," I mumbled out loud as I silently told him, "Oh sure, you can handle fifty or sixty street-savvy pit bulls, Rottweilers, and German shepherds, but let's see you try to get control of this motley crew." I told the dogs, "Thank you," as I went to see who was here.

The truck and trailer were sitting directly in front of the house. The truck was a Chevy, built back when car manufacturers were still putting in those small, triangle-shaped wing windows that you could open for ventilation and direct the flow of air. It probably hadn't been a very fancy truck, even when it was new. It didn't appear as though it had been purchased with many extras. But it did look as if it had served its owner well. Dents along the side of the bed had begun to rust. The dark blue paint on the bottom had faded, nearly matching the powder blue color of the top. The wide strips of chrome that separated the two-tone paint were mostly missing. A jagged crack ran diagonally across the back window.

I could see an elderly man sitting behind the wheel. He was by himself, and he sat stoically, looking straight ahead. I didn't notice him turn his head to watch the house, as though waiting to see if someone might emerge. I walked out the back door and went to greet him. He must have seen me out of the corner of his eye. He opened the driver's side door and got out of his truck.

He was a very small man, made even more so from being stooped with age. He wore a ball cap on his head and was dressed in pin-stripped overalls over a denim work shirt. His brown leather boots were scuffed and dirty. There was several days' worth of gray stubble on his chin. He shuffled unsteadily as he walked to meet me. I instinctively quickened my pace to shorten the gap between us.

I was about to ask, "May I help you?" I thought perhaps he was lost and had pulled in for directions. But I never got the words out. The elderly man spoke first.

"Can you take this horse?" He made eye contact with me briefly, but quickly directed his gaze to the trailer behind his truck. You couldn't see that a horse was inside. At one time the rusty stock trailer had been spray painted a dark blue to match the truck. But now the paint was flaking off. It was as old and dilapidated as the truck pulling it. There was plywood screwed to the bars of the sidewalls. That was why I hadn't seen the horse. And whoever was inside was standing very still and had not even raised its head.

I started to respond, but I didn't really know what to say, so I closed my mouth. I was just a bit surprised that anyone in our new town already knew we took in horses. And I was even more surprised that someone would just pull in without calling, with a horse in tow. What if no one had been home? And I was perplexed how he even found us.

The man turned back to face me when I did not answer him. I was about to ask him all of these questions I had as we looked at each other. But I saw tears filling his eyes and so, once again, I remained quiet.

"I can't take care of her no more," he said, breaking the silence. His voice was unsteady and his chin quivered as he said the words. He put a rough and weathered hand over his mouth and looked back at the trailer as he wiped his eyes. It is not uncomfortable for me to be around someone who is emotional over an animal, even when it's a man. I understand the tears we shed for them and feel genuine empathy. And I do not usually have trouble finding something comforting to say. But for some reason, it seemed better for me to simply remain quiet. And so I said nothing.

The old man reached out to steady himself against the side of the truck. His hand smeared the dust as it slid along and he shuffled toward the back of the trailer. He paused suddenly and glanced in my direction. "You'll take her," he said. I couldn't tell if it was a question or a statement. But I found myself nodding.

He reached the back end of the trailer and unlatched the bar with some difficulty. He slowly pushed the door open. I was inclined to step forward and help, but remained standing where

I was. I heard the mare nicker to him and finally saw her lift her head above the plywood as she turned around to face him. I could hear him speaking to her in a soothing tone of voice, but was unable to make out what he was saying. I heard him clip the lead rope onto her halter, and then he encouraged the horse to step out of the trailer. She did as he asked, and then quietly stood by his side.

She was a small horse, no more than fourteen hands. Her coat was chestnut-colored, and she had a flaxen mane and tail. I could tell that she was elderly; the hollows above her eyes were quite pronounced, her back was beginning to sway, and there were traces of gray hair all around her face. But she looked in fair condition. And it appeared that she had just been brushed. Her coat was shiny, and her mane and tail were free from tangles. Even her feet had recently been trimmed.

The old man and his horse made their way around the trailer. He kept one hand on her neck, and the other held the lead rope. One small tug of her head would have made him lose his balance, but she was a quiet little mare and walked gently by his side. He came to stand in front of me and reached forward with the horse's lead rope. I took the tail end, but he didn't release his grasp. I looked up and met his gaze. Tears filled his eyes once more, but he didn't look away. I brought my chin down, almost imperceptibly nodding at him. He finally looked away and turned to the horse.

The air seemed to change, or maybe it was the atmosphere, but the old man behaved as if I were no longer standing there. He put his open palm up to the mare's cheek. His fingertips were feather light and barely brushed her hair. He touched her lightly along her muzzle and made his way up to her eyes, feeling all the contours of her face. He laced his fingers through her mane and stepped even closer to her.

"I can't take care of you no more, girl," he whispered. "I can't take care of you." His tears fell freely and rolled down his cheeks.

He tipped his forehead against her neck and looked down at the ground. Once again he rubbed a shaking hand over his mouth. I swallowed hard and put my head down. Then the old man simply turned away and went to his truck. Before he opened the door he looked back in my direction.

"She was a good horse," he told me. I bit my lower lip and then squeezed my eyes shut for just a second as I nodded at him. I couldn't bear the sadness on his face. Without another word, he climbed into the driver's seat and started his truck. He circled around and then pulled back out of our driveway.

The old mare and I stood beside each other and watched him leave. I felt immobilized for a moment, but then he was gone from sight and I turned to look her. "You're going to be okay, girl," I said. My own voice sounded odd to me, and I suddenly realized that I had not said anything to him. I hadn't uttered a single word.

I also realized that he hadn't told me her name. "What's your name, sweetheart?" I asked her. She didn't answer; just stared back at me calmly as she waited to see what was next. I ran my hand down her neck. "How about we call you Granny?" It seemed to suit her and she didn't seem to mind her new name. I turned around and started walking her back to a small ten-acre pasture we had for our elderly horses.

"C'mon, Granny. Let's go meet the other old folks. I think you're gonna like it here."

Liberty

THERE WAS A LIGHT RAP ON MY BEDROOM DOOR. I was in that in-between state of being half awake and half asleep. I wasn't really sure if I heard someone knocking, or if I had dreamed it.

"Mel?" It was Sarah's husband, Stephen.

I sat up in bed. "Yeah."

"Sorry to bother you," he said through the door. "But you've got company."

"What! Someone's here?" I reached for my glasses that were sitting on the night stand and looked over at the clock. "It's seven o'clock in the morning," I called out. Stephen remained quiet. I pushed the covers back and got out of bed. "I thought I heard the dogs barking," I mumbled to myself as I threw on some sweat-pants and went to open the bedroom door. "Who is it?" I asked him.

"Um, well . . . I can't really answer that." Stephen said. "I don't know who it is. You better just come see." I studied him for just a second through narrowed eyes. He had an odd expression

on his face; sort of a cross between being highly amused and just
a little perplexed.

"What are you trying to pull?" I asked.

"Me!" he exclaimed. "Why would you say that?"

"'Cause I know you. What's with the smirk?"

"I'm innocent. Just c'mon." Stephen led the way into the
kitchen, out through the garage, and then he pushed open the
overhead door. We stepped out to stand in the driveway. He
glanced back at me and made a slight gesture, pointing in the
direction of the front gate. With the hint of a spreading grin on
his face he waited for my reaction to who was standing there.

"What the—" I said. "Where the heck did *he* come from?" I
ran both my hands through my mussed hair, sort of pulling it at
the same time as I laced my fingers together over the top of my
head. I tried to think about what to do next. I looked back at
Stephen with my elbows sticking out like elephant ears. His smirk
had now developed into a full-fledged grin.

"You think this is funny!" I said. I looked back towards the
front gate.

Stephen glanced over at me and opened his mouth to speak.
He seemed to rethink what he was about to say when he saw the
expression on my face and closed his mouth. Then he looked
back over at the gate, crossed his arms over his chest in a decisive
manner, and started nodding, his mirth over the situation finally
winning out. "Yeah," he said. He was nodding vigorously now.
"Yeah, I do."

I unlaced my fingers and let my hands drop down to my
sides. "Oh, my," I said. Suddenly I started laughing. "Where's
Sarah?" I asked.

"She was in the shower, but she should be out by now."

"Does she know?" I asked.

"Nope," Stephen said.

"I better go tell her," I said.

"Oh no," Stephen said. "Allow me." He turned on his heel.
The wide grin on his face settled back down to an indiscernible

smirk. It would be more fun for him to downplay who was standing at the front gate and wait for her reaction, just as he had done with me. I smiled as I watched him return to the house. I was struck by how grateful I was that he and Sarah were here.

• • •

Jim and I were still living in Florida when my niece Sarah and her husband Stephen met. We loved him immediately. He was incredibly kind and thoughtful and had a hilarious sense of humor. He could easily bust me up with laughter, and he and I had developed a bantering relationship that was based on mutual admiration. Stephen earned his living as a CPA, and Sarah was still managing a large feed store at the time. While they were dating they would frequently come out to our house on the weekends to help with some of the bigger tasks around Proud Spirit. We were thrilled when Stephen asked Sarah to marry him.

I was excited and happy when Sarah asked me to stand up with her as part of her wedding party. We began excitedly making plans. The day Sarah and I went to look at wedding dresses was especially poignant. The sales clerk helped us haul armloads of flowing white gowns into the enormous dressing room. I waited in the mirrored outer room while Sarah put the first one on.

"Ready," she called out to me before opening the door. When she emerged I was overwhelmed with emotion. I could not have felt more happiness for her if she were my own child. I couldn't even speak as I looked at how remarkably beautiful she was in that gown. I simply started crying instead.

Unfortunately, Sarah and Stephen's wedding plans were intermingled with plans for them to move out of state. The company Stephen worked for offered him a position in Tennessee that he did not want to turn down. I was, of course, horrified.

After they moved, Jim and I managed to get away and visit them in their new home. And they came back to Florida as often as they could. But it wasn't the same. Sarah had been an enormous part of my life and I hated living so far apart.

Life went on, and eventually our own move to the new facility in Arkansas brought us a little closer together geographically. The drive between Sarah and Stephen's place and ours was now only eight hours. Whenever Stephen could get away from work they came to stay with us. And every now and then Sarah was able to come on her own for more frequent visits. From their very first visit with us they had both remarked how much they loved the area. And so we all kept having conversations about one day living closer together again.

One evening the phone rang. It was Sarah. "Hey, we're thinking about coming for a long weekend."

"Great," I said.

"Yeah," she said casually. "We have an appointment with a realtor."

This was such a shock, it didn't really register. "What? Here? Wh-what do you mean," I sputtered.

"We're moving!" Sarah said. "We're moving to Mena!"

"What!" I put my hand over my mouth and, of course, started crying.

I had no idea that Sarah and Stephen had been keeping their eyes open for a business for sale. They wanted to surprise us. Or avoid disappointment if nothing ever came along that might be the right venture for them. Miraculously, an established CPA practice in town had just come up for sale. Stephen had found the ad on the internet and had already spoken at length with the owner. They had a meeting with her that weekend, plus they were getting together with a realtor to look at several ranches for sale with enough acreage for Sarah's five horses.

Sarah and Stephen arrived that weekend to finalize the contract and purchase the CPA business. They'd had a long and tiring couple days with the realtor. None of the homes or properties they looked at were anything they wanted to pursue. Jim and I told them not to worry. If they hadn't found anything when it came time to move, they could stay with us till the right place came along. It was Sunday evening and they were heading back to Tennessee in the morning to tie up loose ends, finish packing, and get things in order for their horses to make the trip to Arkansas.

The phone rang while the four of us were sitting out in the front yard, watching the sunset. It was the realtor. She asked to speak to Sarah or Stephen. Sarah took the call.

"There's a place that just came on the market that she wants us to see before we leave in the morning," Sarah said when she joined us back outside. "They haven't even put the sign up yet."

"Where is it?" I asked.

"She said it's a cute little home on forty acres," Sarah said.

"Where?"

Sarah looked up with a huge smile on her face. "It's right around the corner."

Sold! In June of 2006 Sarah and Stephen moved to Mena. They immediately went to work establishing the CPA practice they had purchased, and were living with us till the mid-July closing date on the new home. And it really was just around the corner. Their land *almost* touches the back side of our property.

If we had orchestrated the perfect scenario for Sarah and Stephen to find a business, sell their home, and find one here near us, it could not have come together any better than it did. I am thrilled that my dreams to have Sarah close to me again have come true.

• • •

Sarah walked out the back door with a towel wrapped around her head. Stephen was bringing up the rear. "Who's here?" she asked. I clasped my hands behind my back and stepped out of her line of vision. She looked past me, in the direction of the driveway. Her eyes grew wide when she saw the pure white donkey standing outside our gate.

"Where in the world did he come from?" she asked. I was

about to answer that I didn't know. But suddenly, as if on cue, the donkey reared up on his back legs and came crashing down on the gate with his two front feet. It made an awful clatter. "Whoa, easy fella," Sarah said with a laugh.

Up until then he had simply been standing there, just looking around, calmly gazing across our property. He looked as gentle as a white puffy cloud. But apparently he had been quietly making his battle plan, and he was now ready to execute it. We watched as he suddenly started pawing at the ground like an enraged bull and then he charged forward to slam his shoulder against the gate. "Hey!" I hollered. The quiet little donkey had turned into a thunderstorm and appeared very angry as he smashed into the gate again, determined to get through.

Biscuit and Liberty saying hello

"You don't know him?" Sarah asked.

"Never seen him before in my life," I said, shaking my head.

"Do you think someone might have just dropped him off?"

"I don't know. It's possible, I guess."

The mad little donkey lifted his head high in the air and slammed into the gate once again. And then he let out an ear-shattering screeching bray that echoed through the hills. Sarah covered her hand with her mouth and we both started laughing. It sounded suspiciously familiar and reminded us of another little maniacal donkey we both knew. And it also snapped me into action.

"Okay," I said. "He was cute when he was just standing there. But he's not so cute anymore. We need to do something." I put my hands on my hips. "Sarah," I said, and nodded in the direction of the assailant.

"What do you mean 'Sarah'?" she asked, just a touch incredulously.

I didn't answer. I just looked from her and then back to the donkey, all while furiously jerking my head in his direction.

"What do you expect *me* to do?" she asked. "We're on our way into work." She waved a hand between her and Stephen. "I'm in dress clothes!" she added.

With perfect timing, Stephen stepped forward and said, "I can manage by myself today, honey. You can stay home with Mel and play with the donkey."

"Yes!" I yelled and started jumping up and down. "You're the best, Stephen."

"Play with the donkey . . . *play!*" Sarah said.

I was still jumping up and down. "I'm gonna go get changed out of my PJs." I quickly glanced at Sarah. "You go get out of your dress clothes and I'll meet you back out here in five minutes."

I breezed by her, but she didn't move. "What," I said, stopping to turn around and look at her. She screwed her mouth to the side. "C'mon!" I said at last. "It'll be fun. We have experience in this sort of thing. We're professionals, so to speak. Remember? We're donkey whisperers." Sarah rolled her eyes.

The donkey was still pawing and smashing himself against the gate. But before I managed to get inside the house to change my clothes there was a sudden lull in the noise he was making. We all stopped and looked in his direction. He had turned away from us and was running up the driveway. I thought maybe he was simply going to leave. I certainly didn't want him loose on the road, but at least he had stopped trying to knock my gate off its hinges. He was almost to the road when he circled back around and faced our property, and then, with a calculated look in his eye he broke into a full gallop.

"Oh my god," I moaned. "What is he doing?"

We all watched in horror as the little white donkey came pounding back down our gravel driveway. I thought surely he was going to break his neck. I clenched my fists, waiting for the wreck. When he came within a few feet of the gate, instead of smashing into it, he shifted his weight and sailed right over. Stephen's eyes were like saucers and Sarah and I stood there with our mouths hanging open.

The little donkey was now in our front yard, but he had no interest in us, nor did he slow down. He ran around in a tight circle till he regained his momentum. In a blur of white, he flattened his foot-long ears back against his head, tucked his tiny little hooves, and effortlessly cleared the fence that was barring him from the pasture. And my horses. He looked like a seasoned Olympic jumper. His form was perfect. Unfortunately, there was a startling revelation when he extended his back legs behind him to clear the fence.

"Oh, no," I wailed to Sarah. "Did you see what I saw?"

"Yep," she nodded.

We could clearly see that the little interloper was "intact." No wonder he had been so determined. The donkey had not been gelded and it was obvious he had romance on his mind. I did not need twenty-plus mares in foal, all giving birth to mules. And he looked like he had the energy to breed every last one of them.

We watched as he ran for the herd, bucking and braying as he went. The horses had noticed the ruckus and they all started running and bucking as well. This was serious.

"Okay," Stephen said, clapping his hands together once. "I guess you two got this covered so I'm gonna head off to work." Sarah and I gave him a wave of dismissal and then we both bolted for the house to change our clothes.

We met back outside and ran to find the herd. They had made their way to a section of the pasture that was situated behind the barn. They were still very agitated, but had stopped running. Now they were flowing as one in a large circle. Most of them were prancing with their tails up and their heads held high as they snorted loud blasts of air through their nostrils over this strange little creature who was now in their midst.

The donkey was a blur of white in a sea of forty-plus sorrel and bay bodies. He galloped from one mare to the next, tossing his head and switching his tail in delight. It seemed as though he was beginning to weave, like a drunken sailor crazed at the prospect of having so many women at his disposal. I could almost hear the rousing tune from the musical *South Pacific*. "There Is Nothing Like a Dame!"

"What do you want to do?" Sarah asked.

"I'm not sure. But if he starts mounting mares I swear I'm gonna shoot him."

"Yeah, right," she said, laughing. "Let's see how approachable he is. We might be able to just halter him and then yank his little hinny outta there."

Sarah took a halter and moved the herd away. But the donkey wouldn't let her anywhere near him.

"How about we start letting the horses into the paddock," she said. "As soon as he follows one of them in, we can work on getting our horses back out. At least we'll have him isolated rather than running the entire property."

We opened the big gate that leads to the paddock near the

barn. I called out to them and a few who were close by came trotting over. We didn't let them through, but waited till more of the horses noticed we were asking them to come in. More of the herd came over. Most were beginning to forget about the disruption out in the pasture. More and more of the herd became interested in what we were doing. Soon they were all milling about, up near the gate.

The donkey came galloping over as well and several of the geldings attempted to kick him or run him off. He was creating quite a disruption. We noticed that he was particularly interested in Pie, one of our older mares. Sarah went into the mix of the herd and shuffled several of them out of the way while we worked to get the group Pie was in closer to the gate. It worked perfectly and we confined five of our horses in the paddock, four geldings and Pie, as well as the offending donkey.

"Let's halter Pie and lead her into the barn. See if we can get him to follow," I said. He did. We secured Pie in a stall and let the donkey romance her from the other side of the stall door. Hopefully, she would keep him entertained and he wouldn't go jumping over any more fences. Sarah returned the four geldings to the pasture while I gave Pie a portion of grain for her graciousness. Then I went in the house to find out where this little troublemaker came from.

Numerous phone calls finally put me in touch with his owner. His name was Shooter Williams and he lived a little over two miles away, down three dirt roads.

"Hmm, wonder what he's doin' all the way down there," Shooter mused after the introductions were made and I had explained the situation. He told me that he knew his donkey was missing, then explained that his property is surrounded by national forest and just assumed he was back in the woods rooting around for acorns. Apparently it wasn't an uncommon occurrence.

"Well, I'm guessing he's looking for companionship," I offered. "I have a lot of mares down here."

"Makes no never-mind," Shooter said. "You'll never catch him, and you can't lead him even if you do. He's wild as a March hare."

"I wasn't planning on catching him or leading him anywhere. I was gonna leave that to you." There was silence on the other end of the line. "He's your donkey." Silence. "You are gonna come get him, aren't you?"

"But that's what I'm tryin' to tell ya. No one can catch him," Shooter replied.

"Well," I chuckled nervously. "We . . . er, *you* gotta do *something*. He hasn't been gelded."

"Yes, ma'am. I know that. That's 'cause he's wild as a March hare and you can't catch him."

"So what are you gonna do?" I asked.

"And even if you do catch him, you can't lead him," he repeated.

"Yes, you already said that. So what are you gonna do?"

"Nothin' we can do," he said.

"I have almost thirty mares here!" I reminded him.

Silence.

"Shooter, I don't need, or want, thirty little donkeys running around here."

"Well, technically, they'd be mules," Shooter interjected.

I snorted out a little gasp of exasperation. "Listen, we have to do something. *You* have to do something. I have him confined in the barn right now. But that's because he's presently enamored with a mare who is locked in a stall. When the thrill is gone, or I need to turn her back out, he's going to jump my fences again and be back out with the herd." I paused and let the air out of my lungs in a dramatic sigh. "I swear," I muttered under my breath, "that damn donkey can fly."

Shooter laughed. "Yes, ma'am. That's how he ended up down at your place."

It may have seemed like the conversation wasn't going very well, or that Shooter was being obstinate, but that wasn't true.

Things like this in life are difficult to describe, and even harder to explain, but I actually liked this guy. We were playing each other like a fish on a line and it occurred to me that if I ever needed the help of a neighbor, I could call on Shooter Williams.

"So . . . what are you gonna do about it?" I asked.

"There's nothin' I can do," he said. "'Cept maybe come down there and shoot him, then drag his sorry butt home."

I didn't react out loud to his comment, but a slight smirk crossed my face. I kept the phone up to my ear as I turned away from the kitchen window I was looking out. I casually leaned back against the counter, waiting. Shooter couldn't see me, of course, but I think he sensed my posture. And he knew that I knew he was kidding. But he couldn't resist trying one more time.

"That is," he said very slowly, "that is, if that's all right with you?" I could hear the smile in his voice.

"If you come down here and shoot him?" I asked casually.

"Yeah. And then, of course, I'd drag his butt home after I shoot him," Shooter concluded.

"His *sorry* butt," I corrected.

"Yeah, his sorry butt."

I paused for just a moment as I contemplated my options. "I just got myself a flying donkey, didn't I?"

Shooter burst out laughing. "Well, I guess maybe you did," he said. "And I ain't even gonna send you a bill."

When I was off the phone with Shooter, I immediately called our vet and made an appointment to have the little donkey gelded. He could come out the following day. We would manage till then. When I put the phone back in the charger, I looked down at the calendar. In a few days it would be the fourth of July.

I walked back out to the barn and Sarah waiting there. The donkey was standing calmly beside Pie's stall and Sarah was petting his neck. She smiled at me when I walked up. "He's not so crazy," she said.

"His owner is," I said and then laughed. "And he doesn't want him back."

"You're kidding." She looked back down at the donkey. "What are we going to do with him?"

"We're gonna get him gelded and then turn him out with the herd," I said. "I named him Liberty, by the way."

Sarah and I pondered over whether or not Shooter had dropped the donkey off here, or if he really did escape and come looking for mares. Either scenario is possible. We really don't know exactly what happened. I don't know why Shooter never had the little donkey gelded or why he didn't want him back. Or why he even had him in the first place. But I don't struggle over these things. I don't question why an animal finds its way to us. It just is what it is, and we just do what we do.

Liberty has been with us almost a year. He was gelded without a problem and has become a happy little part of our herd. And he's never tried to escape.

Rosie and Cracker

ROSIE AND CRACKER WERE TWO MARES WHO WERE DEEPLY BONDED to each other. Naturally, we had seen these close attachments among many of our horses. Anyone who has spent any time at all around horses has seen the tell-tale behavior, and it was evident with Rosie and Cracker. They moved as one. Even when they stood under a shade tree some parts of their bodies were always touching, and when they grazed they practically nibbled on the same blade of grass.

But these two mares went beyond the typical behavior of closely bonded horses and appeared to be in a league of their own. We had never seen anything quite like them. As though they possessed an unspoken power to read each other's mind, they reacted to any given situation at exactly the same moment, in exactly the same way. It was uncanny.

Rosie and Cracker also disliked being anywhere near the rest of the herd. But they didn't just amble off when another horse came too close. They actually galloped off in their quest to keep

As they keep their distance from the herd, Rosie stands protectively over Cracker.

other horses at bay, and they didn't stop until they were at the other side of the pasture. Many times we had observed Rosie and Cracker quietly grazing, off on their own away from the herd. If another horse happened to wander nearby, they would suddenly look up in perfect harmony at the approaching horse, viciously pin all four ears, kick out in the direction of the intruder, and then take off—again, all in perfect harmony. It was as if their display of irritation were a choreographed dance. I regarded them as somewhat of an anomaly. It wasn't normal.

I even ended up giving them a collective nickname: Greta and Garbo. I didn't really assign which one of them was Greta or who was Garbo, but it was clear to the rest of us that (spoken in a deep, gravelly voice with a bad Swedish accent) "they vant to be alone."

Rosie came to us when she was approximately nine years old.

She was a lovely red roan Tennessee Walker. Up until the time she came to Proud Spirit, Rosie's life had consisted of numerous owners and various trainers trying to ride her, and for her part, Rosie had devoted herself to furiously bucking them right back off. She had been owned by rough and tough cowboys who tried to "break" her, and by gentle women who tried to "connect" with her. She had been "whispered" to and "shown who was boss." No one ever had a successful ride on her. No one. She had caused more than one broken bone, and even put one woman in the hospital.

There were plenty of fairly callous suggestions about what should be done with the irascible mare. The kindest suggestion was that she should be sold to a rodeo as premium bucking stock, but that's no life for a horse. The final person in her chain of owners recognized that not every horse should be ridden. After her cast was removed, the woman contacted Proud Spirit about letting Rosie live out her life at our sanctuary. We agreed to provide her with a home where she would never have to contend with removing a rider from her back.

On the day she arrived, we turned her out with the herd of thirty-plus horses we had at that time. Sadly, Rosie wandered off by herself and never formed a relationship with any of the others. Day after day we saw her standing alone.

Cracker was an older mare who came to us shortly after Rosie arrived. She belonged to a couple who loved the horse dearly and took wonderful care of her. They had recently made the difficult decision to give up their life and home in the country for family commitments and move back into town. Cracker needed a new home. Her full name was Golden Graham Cracker. She was a lovely golden Palomino. She had no health problems, other than the fact that she was getting older and she needed to retire. Cracker was twenty-three when she arrived at Proud Spirit. We turned her out in our large pasture the day she arrived. We watched as she veered away from the herd and then settled in a corner to graze by herself.

We will never know exactly what drew them together, but very soon we saw that Rosie and Cracker had become one. My two little spinsters, Greta and Garbo, spent the next seven years at each other's side. Nearly a year after we were settled at the new farm in Arkansas, I began to have concerns about what would happen to Rosie when Cracker was gone. They were over fifteen years apart in age. We would most likely lose Cracker first. I worried about how Rosie would cope.

That heartbreaking day came in the spring of 2006. It was my normal routine to go for a walk around the property every day and check on the herd. Our pastures and the grass were so sufficient that we no longer brought the herd into the barn for grain. One day I could not find Rosie and Cracker. It was normal that they would be off on their own, but scanning the property, I was unable to locate them. I continued walking our hills and finally crested a ridge when I spotted them down in a valley. At first I was not alarmed. Cracker was lying down in the tall grass, as Rosie calmly stood over her beloved herd mate. She appeared to be dozing as well. Her head was hanging low and one back leg was cocked in repose. I made my way down to them and before I even drew near, within seconds, I realized that Cracker had died.

On impulse, I rushed to her side, even though there was nothing I could do. As I approached, I reached for Rosie's neck and tangled my fingers in her thick red mane. "Oh, Rosie," I cried looking down at Cracker's lifeless body. "What happened, girl?" I kneeled down beside Cracker and lifted her head onto my lap. "Oh, I'm so sorry, Cracker," I told her through my tears. "You were such a good girl. You were so good to Rosie." I smoothed her forelock and cupped my hand over her eye to shut it. There was no sign of trauma or a struggle. It appeared that Cracker's time had simply come. Rosie stood at Cracker's side, looking down at me, just blinking slowly.

I lifted Cracker's head from my lap and tucked her chin down near her chest. I ran my fingers through her forelock one last time and closed her other eyelid. Next, I scooted around to her legs and tucked them near her belly and then pulled her tail back close to her body. I remained on my knees and shut my eyes. I was crying and did not speak out loud, but I told Cracker I loved her a final time and then I said good-bye.

I got to my feet and went to Rosie's side. "I don't know how you're going to handle this, sweet girl," I said. My heart was breaking for her. I sighed heavily and then turned to go tell Jim.

I do not doubt that horses grieve. Although there are experts who say they don't, I would never believe it, ever. I'd seen too much of it. But I wondered what horses understood about death and dying. Did Rosie realize that Cracker would never get up? Was she absorbing the grim reality of this situation as it unfolded in front of her?

Jim and I are very conscientious, to the best of our ability, about giving our horses the life they would have without man's interference. Of course, we tend to their needs and provide veterinary and farrier care whenever it is required. We devote our lives to their well-being and do not hold back treatment to ensure that they are healthy and taken care of. But I do not believe in constantly interfering with or redirecting the natural way events in life occur. That includes the grieving process. We allowed Rosie time to stand over Cracker before we buried her.

Later that afternoon Jim took the tractor out to where Cracker had died. I followed on foot, carrying a halter in case I needed to move Rosie away while Jim dug the hole. I hoped that I wouldn't need the halter. I hoped that Rosie would have moved away on her own by now. But as we crested the hill, I could see that she was still keeping vigil over Cracker's body. With tears in my eyes I slipped the halter over Rosie's head and walked her about fifty yards away while Jim laid Cracker to rest.

Over the next four days, I made the very same trek along our hills and continued to check on Rosie. Each time I found her in the exact same spot, standing over the last place she saw her beloved companion. I always went to her side and spent a little time with her, but she was not interested in me or my attempts to soothe her.

On the fifth day, I made the decision to bring Rosie up and confine her near the house. I was concerned she was not drinking enough water. She did not fret or argue about leaving the valley, and allowed me to lead her up to the barn. We saw her drinking and grazing normally in the paddock where I placed her. We kept her in for seven days.

After that entire week had passed, I felt sure that Rosie would now somehow integrate into the herd. I went out to her and walked her to the gate. We stood together for just a moment. "You need to go with the others now," I said. "It's time to make new friends." She stood looking out over the pasture. I reached up and removed the halter. She moved away from me, and then, with pounding hooves, she ran at breakneck speed back to where Cracker lay. I was heartbroken as I watched her crest the hill and angle toward the valley. I swallowed hard over the lump of sadness in my throat and made a mental note to check on her later.

That afternoon I walked outside and scanned the herd. I searched for Rosie's unique roan coat among the sorrel, bay, and painted ponies of our herd, hoping she was with them. It was in vain. She wasn't there.

I turned in the direction of the valley and started walking to the place where I knew she stood. As I crested the hill, I found Rosie standing with her head down beside the bare patch of dirt. But something remarkable had happened. She wasn't alone. Ranger, our beautiful boy who had saved all those babies, had left the herd and was standing by Rosie's side. I glanced around to see if any other horses were nearby, but Rosie and Ranger were completely by themselves. It was impossible! Ranger couldn't go anywhere without two or three babies dogging his every move.

It was even more extraordinary to me that these two horses had been pastured together for years and they had never even come within twenty feet of one another. What had compelled this remarkable gelding to sense that Rosie was alone, down in a valley that was not even visible from where the herd had been grazing? I was dumbstruck by what I was witnessing. And I was in awe of Ranger's intuition and everything we will never be able to comprehend about animals.

We watched throughout that day and the next as Ranger gently eased Rosie away from the place where Cracker had died. He quietly grazed as he moved a few feet each hour. Rosie calmly moved along with him until she was back in the security of the herd. She remained by his side for a few more days, and then formed a strong friendship with Rebel and Gambler, two geldings who were thick as thieves. And now they were three. After that time we never saw Rosie and Ranger anywhere near each other again. We believe he understood that she needed to be back with the herd. And now that she was, his work with Rosie was done.

Rebel

"HEY, TAKE A LOOK AT THIS LETTER that just came in the mail," I said to Jim as I breezed into his den waving an envelope. He was sitting at his desk concentrating intently on something on his computer screen.

"What is it?" he asked without redirecting his gaze.

"It's from some woman outside of Little Rock," I said. "She wants me to come over there to look at her horse."

"Yeah," Jim said, still peering at the monitor.

"Well, just read it," I asked. "It's sorta weird. See what you think."

Jim leaned back in his chair, took the envelope from my hand, and removed the contents.

"Ugh," he grimaced, leafing through the three long hand-written pages. "Can't you give me the Reader's Digest version?"

"Well, her name is Dana and she sounds a little pleading, or desperate, or something," I said. I took the letter back out of Jim's hand and sat down on the couch. Jim swiveled his chair around

*Rebel, now part
of the herd*

to face me. "She starts out by saying that they're having some serious problems with their horse. And she says that she's writing to
'warn' me," I looked up at Jim and pointed at the ceiling, "warn
me, mind you," I repeated, "that her husband is planning to
phone here to speak with me about the horse. But then she asks
me to please not mention that she wrote." I looked up at Jim.
"Doesn't that seem a little odd?"

"Yeah," Jim shrugged, "but who knows what people are
thinking. What does she say is wrong with the horse?"

"She just says that he has some dangerous behavioral problems. The crux of it is that she thinks the horse needs some sort
of emotional therapy." My head snapped up once again from
looking down at the letter on my lap. "Those were her words," I
said. I was now pointing my finger at Jim's chest. He laughed,
catching my drift. I didn't want him teasing me about horses on
psychiatrists' couches interpreting ink spots.

(My mind wandered momentarily as I envisioned the scene:
Voice of the therapist: "Now Mr. Dobbin, what comes to mind
when you look at this ink spot?" Mr. Dobbin: "The star on my
dam's forehead the day she told me she wasn't in love with my
sire." Therapist: "And this?" Mr. Dobbin: "The star on the fore-

head of the horse who kicked me when I was just a yearling."
Therapist: "And this?" Mr. Dobbin: "The star on the forehead of
that nasty little mare I tried to befriend who told me she had
never seen such lousy cow-hocked crappy conformation."
Therapist nodding: "I see . . . very interesting.")

I shook my head and returned to the letter on my lap, "But
she says that her husband insists the horse is a rogue and needs to
be put down."

"A rogue, huh," Jim said and furrowed his brow. "What
exactly does she mean by rogue?"

"She said he's tried to kill her. Numerous times."

"And just what does she want you to do?"

"She says she wants me to evaluate him and mediate what
action they'll take." I put my hands out in front of me, palms facing the ceiling as I weighed them up and down. "Emotional therapy . . . euthanasia . . . emotional therapy . . . euthanasia," I
chanted.

Jim laughed. "Yeah, like you'd actually have to think about
that one. So what exactly is emotional therapy for horses anyway?" he asked.

"Got me. I'm guessing she just means that he needs some
retraining or some higher understanding. But whatever it is, I
think I'll opt to encourage the husband to pursue that route
rather than euthanasia."

"So you're gonna go over there?" Jim asked.

"Sure. Why not, if it'll keep a perfectly good horse from being
sent to the guillotine."

Two weeks later I made the three-hour drive over to Little
Rock. Glen Murphy, Dana's husband, did indeed call just as she
said he would. I didn't really see what she needed to warn me
about. He didn't exactly offer much information. The only thing
I gleaned from our conversation was that this seemed to be more
about humoring his wife than actually talking about what solutions there might be to the problems they're having with the
horse.

I easily found the address he had given me. It was located down the winding, tree-lined street of an equestrian community of estate homes. I could see elaborate horse trailers with all the bells and whistles parked beside expansive barns. Here and there horses were grazing peacefully on the lush pastures.

To say that the home of Glen and Dana Murphy was palatial was putting it mildly. The elegant two-story Tudor sat nestled in the middle of thirty manicured acres, all tucked behind three-board wood fencing that had been stained black. The asphalt driveway formed a Y in the direction of the house to the left, and to the barn to the right. I noticed a man stepping out of the wide center door of the barn. He must have seen or heard my truck as I pulled in. He waved for me to come forward and park in a graveled area adjacent to the barn.

"Glen Murphy," he said as he grasped my hand. "You must be Melanie. Thanks for doing this." He was a nice-looking man in his early forties. He was wearing tan riding breeches with dark brown leather patches at the inside of the knees. His stylish black leather boots gleamed in the sun.

I had barely managed a response when he motioned for me to follow him into the barn. It was an immaculate building, and nearly as palatial as the house. The concrete aisleway had been swept clean and it was wide enough to drive a dually pickup truck down without coming anywhere near the sides. There were three wagon-wheel benches set at even intervals along the wall and everything was neat and orderly. There were four closed doors, two on our right and two on our left. They were more than likely a feed and tack room, and perhaps a bathroom and an office. At the other end I could see eight very large stalls. The barn was way bigger than my house.

"Dana's still up at the house," Glen was saying. "I wanted to speak with you in private for a moment, before she comes down."

"Okay," I nodded. I thought about Dana's letter, which she had sent without his knowledge and it struck me that maybe these two should be talking to each other, rather than a stranger behind each other's backs. I would, of course, honor Dana's request and not mention the letter she had sent. It was not my place or inclination to cause trouble, but I had a strange feeling about this couple and already felt uncomfortable.

"This has been terribly upsetting for her," Glen said. "She's crying all the time about this damn horse." He thrust his chin in the direction of the stalls. I turned slightly but didn't see a horse poking his head over the stall door. Glen stepped closer to me and stuck his hands on his hips. "Now listen. She's read that book of yours and is convinced that you'll be able to fix this horse."

I didn't like the way he had gotten in my space and I took a step back as I raised my hand in the universal sign for "stop." "Um, let's slow down a little," I said. "I don't even know what sort of problems you're having. And I wouldn't begin to claim I can fix anything until I know what's wrong."

"My wife begged me to call you. She must have had a reason," Glen stated. "What kind of trainer are you?"

"I'm not a trainer," I told him. "I run a sanctuary for abused horses. I'm good at helping horses learn to trust again, and accept being touched, and become willing partners." I was going to add one other thing, but changed my mind. When someone tells me they have a difficult or "stubborn" horse, or the horse is hard to catch, the problem is usually not the horse at all. It's the person and their lack of knowledge in communicating with horses. Consequently, their horse doesn't want to be with them. I'm good at helping people decipher counter-productive body language and how it is impacting their horse in a negative way, compounding the problem. That is, providing they are open and receptive to looking at their own behavior. I could already see that Glen was more than likely a huge part of the problem and I hadn't even met the horse. He was aggressive in an angry, nervous way, and very domineering. He would not be open to hearing that he was more than likely the problem.

"Regardless," Glen said, dismissing what I just said to him.

"The horse doesn't need a trainer. We've been through four of them."

"And what have they told you?" I asked.

Glen dropped his hands from his hips and narrowed his eyes. "That the horse is dangerous," he said through a tightened jaw. "That if Dana continues to ride him she's going to be seriously injured or killed."

"But are they saying he's dangerous for Dana to ride because he's too much horse for her riding skills? How experienced is she? Or is it because the horse needs more under-saddle training? Maybe more ground work?" I asked.

"The horse is dangerous," he repeated, as though I were a six-year-old who was having trouble understanding something.

I pursed my lips and nodded.

"And that's why I want him put down." His eyes bored into mine. "And that is what I feel you should tell Dana. That it's for the best. She will be able to reconcile herself to this if it comes from you."

I stared back at him with unwavering eyes. I spent nearly twenty years of my life as a firefighter, often the only female in a station full of men whose favorite pastime was trying to intimidate the women. I became adept at not letting that happen and it evolved into a challenging and fun sport for me, and for the men as well, I imagine.

"I have this funny personality quirk," I told Glen. I had not taken my eyes from his and I was smiling sweetly. "I don't like to be told what to do. I have not spoken to Dana yet. Nor have I even seen the horse. Let's just take this a step at a time. Okay?"

For just a moment Glen didn't move. And then he began to nod, ever so slowly. A smile crept along his mouth, but it wasn't a cheerful expression. His smile broadened as his nodding became more vigorous. His eyes were still on me as he backed up in the direction of one of the closed doors. He turned away from me and pushed the button of an intercom system that was mounted on the outside wall.

"Dana," he spoke into the machine. "Come down here."

You jerk, I thought to myself.

Dana Murphy was a beautiful woman. She appeared to be in her late twenties, considerably younger than Glen. She was tall and willowy with lovely brunette hair, which she had pulled back into a neat and tidy pony tail. She was clutching a copy of my first book, *The Horses of Proud Spirit,* to her chest. There were tears swimming in her big brown eyes. She went directly to Glen's side and he slipped an arm possessively around her slender waist.

"Dana, honey," he said. "This is Melanie." He nodded in my direction. He said my name as if there were thorns attached. We clearly did not like each other. "Melanie, this is my wife, Dana."

"I'm so happy to meet you," I said as I reached for her hand. She startled me by stepping forward and grabbing me in a tight hug. I quickly recovered and returned the hug to pat her back. I felt her shudder with a few quick sobs.

"Thank you for coming," she cried as she still held onto me. She finally leaned away, but did not look me in the eyes. "I'm so sorry. I'm so emotional about this."

"It's okay," I said. "I understand. I think I cry about one horse or another what seems like every single day of my life."

"I know," she said. She held the copy of my book up, obviously referring to how often I describe my tears in the collection of stories. We both started laughing. "Would you like to sit down?" Dana indicated one of the wagon-wheel benches and she and I sat down together. Glen leaned back against a wall and crossed his arms over his chest.

"Why don't you tell me about your horse," I said to Dana.

She immediately broke into a radiant smile. She took a deep breath. "Well," she sighed through her smile, "his name is Topaz. Glen bought him for me when we were in Hawaii." She glanced up at her husband and continued, "We were there—"

"We were there on vacation," Glen interrupted. I took my eyes from Dana and glared at him with a slight look of irritation on my face over the fact that he was talking. He did not appear to notice, which I felt was unfortunate. "Dana wanted to go horseback riding on the beach," he continued. "I found a rental place and off we went. When we returned to the stables there was a white horse in a paddock."

"He took my breath away," Dana said.

"He was running with his head up, taking these amazingly long strides. His mane hung below his neck and it was just flying. So was his tail. He had these massive muscles along his chest and legs. I've never seen such a beautiful animal in my life." Glen let out a little chuckle. "I remember looking over at Dana. She really did look like he had taken her breath away. I said 'do you want him, honey?' All she could do was nod." He laughed again and shrugged casually. "So I bought him."

I raised my eyebrows. "Did you ride him or learn anything about his training beforehand?"

"Not really," Dana said. "We just—"

"I paid thirty thousand dollars for that horse," Glen broke in. "And damn near that much to have him shipped to the mainland. For that kind of money he should know how to saddle himself." I sat there dumbfounded, for numerous reasons. But the two that were uppermost in my mind were the fact that someone would pay that much money for a horse they knew nothing about. And that someone would think they will have an obedient horse based solely on the amount of money they paid. I needed a distraction.

I looked at Dana. "Why don't you introduce me to Topaz?" She did not move, but instead looked at Glen, as though asking for permission. He ignored her and struck off for the other end of the barn. "He's right down here," he said.

The three of us walked to the farthest end of the barn. I peered into the last stall. A horse stood with his rear facing the door and his head hanging low. I thought it extremely odd that he had not come to poke his head over the door the entire time we were talking. He wasn't white, as Glen had said. He was a blue roan. This is a shade of gray that is so rich it appears to have tinges of blue in it. His breeding was Andalusian and he was huge.

"Hey, you," I said. "Why are you sulking in the corner?" I put my hand on the door latch and slid it back.

"He never faces out," Glen told me. "I have no idea why. Every trainer we've had in here couldn't get him to face them when they walked into the stall. You have to use a crop or something to get him to turn around."

I stepped into the stall and made a single sharp snapping sound with my tongue against the roof of my mouth. The horse immediately turned around. I relaxed my posture, angled my shoulders away from him, and backed up just a little, inviting him into my space. The horse walked over, sniffing me up and down. I reached for the leather halter with his personalized brass nameplate that was hanging on a hook and slipped it over his head.

"I don't believe this. What did you do?" Glen asked.

"I made like a carrot," I said without further explanation. I had no doubt in my mind that Dana plied this horse full of treats, primarily carrots, evidenced by the five-pound bag sitting on one of the benches. And giving treats is fine in my book. I do the same with my own horses and don't believe for one second that it causes behavioral problems. But it was fairly simple to deduce that this horse knew what a carrot cracking in half sounded like. I let him finish smelling me and then led him out of his stall.

"He has to go in cross ties," Glen said. "It's impossible to do anything with him unless he's tied." He tried to step between me and the horse as he quickly reached for the restraints so he could clip them to the horse's halter to prohibit him from moving about.

I stayed where I was and blocked Glen's movement. "I don't want him in cross ties," I said.

"Why?" he scowled. "We always put him in cross ties."

"How can I see how he reacts to things if he's not allowed to react?"

"Suit yourself," Glen said. He remained in my space and was hovering too close.

"May I ask that you and Dana go sit on one of the benches? I'd like to interact with Topaz without additional input."

They obliged. I completely tuned them out and focused on Topaz. I spent the next twenty minutes fussing over him and just asking him to do simple things, all while he was at liberty: lift all four feet, yield to pressure, allow me to touch his ears, close both his eyes at the same time, put my fingers in his mouth, touch his sheath, and lift his tail. I gently pressed my fingers into his belly, asking him to arch his back. I lifted his chin till his nose pointed toward the sky, and I brought his head down till it was almost between his knees. I asked him to stay out of my space with a slight wave of my hand and he remained still with a gentle tug on the lead rope. He was a playful and engaged horse. And he was a perfect gentleman.

I looked at Dana. "Tell me what he's like under saddle."

"Well," she sighed. "I just wanted him for trail riding. He seems like he's going along fine and then suddenly, I don't know what happens—"

"He starts bucking to get her off his back," Glen said.

"Are you sure he's actually bucking, or is it more like crow-hopping?"

"That's what the trainers have said, he's jigging sideways, not bucking," Dana said.

"He's bucking," Glen snapped. "But whatever you want to call it, he won't let her ride him. And she's going to get hurt. Or worse. The last time it happened Dana was thrown to the ground and he turned around and tried to stomp on her. He went after her and tried to kill her."

I quickly looked at Dana. She avoided my eyes, but shook her head "no." The horse certainly may have been stomping around, and Dana absolutely could have been seriously injured. But to say that the horse was intentionally going after her was ridiculous.

"Can you think of anything that might have startled him that day?" I asked.

Dana nodded. "The neighbor's dogs ran out."

"They didn't come anywhere near us," Glen said.

"But I could tell he was scared."

"Why would he be scared?" Glen snapped. "He weighs a thousand pounds more than a stupid dog. Is it too much to ask of him that we go on a peaceful trail ride?"

It never ceases to amaze me how little some people who own horses actually know about them. But I kept my voice level. "Glen, horses are prey animals. A carnivore running at him is every reason in the world for concern. He has to trust you and Dana. If he is not desensitized to things outside of his comfort zone, then jigging and crow-hopping are completely normal reactions for a horse that's scared," I said.

Glen ignored me and began ranting. "I mean look at this barn. This is a half-million-dollar barn. We've given him everything. He has a custom stall. He gets clean shavings every single day. The flooring is padded underneath. I even had the damn walls padded. He gets top-of-the-line grain, expensive supplements, and all the damn treats he can eat. And this is what we get. This is how he behaves." Glen was breathing heavily. Dana had begun to cry.

As though his words alone weren't absurd beyond belief, they were made even more so by the fact that the horse was politely standing there. He had lots of energy, but he did not have behavioral problems. And it was quite clear that Topaz and I, and possibly Dana, were all thinking the same thing: this guy really is a jerk.

"Glen," I said and put my hands up for him to stop. "Are you serious? Listen to what you're saying. Do you really think this horse cares if he has matching water buckets? He doesn't care about all this." I waved my hand around the barn. "You can't keep a powerful, athletic young horse in a stall all day and then expect him to be a gentle trail horse on the weekends. He needs to be exposed to things, he needs to develop confidence, to move around, and exert some energy, be with other horses and graze. He needs to be allowed to be a horse. You aren't giving him *anything* he needs."

"Four trainers," he shouted. "We've had four trainers in here who can't tell us what's wrong with him."

"That's because there *is* nothing wrong with him," I said. "Have you listened to anything I just said? Did you listen to the trainers? Did you ever think that maybe he's too much horse for Dana's riding ability? Maybe he's not the right match for her? Maybe you shouldn't have bought him without knowing anything about him." Out of the corner of my eye I saw Dana lift her head. She had been staring down at her lap, wringing her hands and quietly crying, but she must have known what was coming.

Apparently I had hit a nerve.

"I did not pay thirty thousand dollars for a horse my wife can't ride!"

No one spoke as Glen's words echoed off the metal walls of his half-million-dollar barn. The only sound was Dana sniffling. It was clear now what had him galled. He was trying to save face by branding the horse a rogue. It wasn't a bad decision on his part to have bought this horse. It wasn't even his pretty wife's fault for not knowing how to ride him. The horse was at fault.

"I'm afraid you did," I said.

Glen turned to Dana. "You have two choices. Convince her," he jerked his thumb in my direction, "to take this horse under the agreement that she signs the papers you and I have already discussed, or we get a vet out here tomorrow and have him put down." He walked out of the barn.

I stood and watched his retreating back. When he disappeared into the garage of the house I turned to Dana. She was still crying. "I don't know what to say," I told her.

"Please, don't say anything." Dana abruptly wiped her eyes. "I'm so sorry. He can be," she paused and shook her head. "He can be difficult."

I sighed heavily, feeling very sorry for her. I decided to just keep my mouth shut, but would have been inclined to offer a different description than "difficult."

Dana explained the papers Glen wanted me to sign. The papers had been drawn up by a lawyer and would be signed in front of a notary public. They stated that Topaz was a dangerous and untrainable horse. Glen Murphy and his estate were absolved from any responsibility if at any time any person should be injured or killed by this rogue horse. He was never to be sold or given away, but instead, he was to be turned free at our facility and remain in the custody of Proud Spirit Horse Sanctuary until the day he dies.

I signed the papers and Topaz came to Proud Spirit. We, of course, gave him a new name: Rebel, with a cause.

The Trouble with Sophie

"OKAY, EINSTEIN. NOW WHAT?" I asked myself out loud as I turned in a circle. I was standing in our driveway holding onto the lead rope of a six-year-old gelding we had just brought to Proud Spirit. He was calmly waiting for direction while I stood clueless beside him, wondering what in the world I was going to do with him.

My eyes wandered from the big main pasture over to a small half-acre paddock up near the house. Next I turned and pondered a larger one-acre paddock that surrounded our barn. And then my eyes scanned the ten-acre pasture behind the barn. It was set up for our elderly horses who didn't do well being turned out with the large herd. That's a possibility, I thought. But what about Sophie? I envisioned her cantankerous attitude and wasn't sure what I should do.

"Are you talking to me?" Jim said. He looked over at me from the back of his truck. We had borrowed Sarah's trailer to bring this new horse home and planned to return it to her later in the

Joe and Sophie

week. After we had unloaded the gelding, Jim had backed the trailer off to the side of the driveway and he was just getting ready to unhitch it.

"No," I laughed. "I'm talking to myself. But your input is welcome. I guess I didn't think this out too well. I'm not sure where to put him." I looked around the property again. And then I looked at the horse who stood calmly by my side.

He was a little over fourteen hands high. Both his mane and tail were long and very thick, and they were just a shade darker than his solid bay coat. His forelock covered up a small, white star between his eyes. Other than that, the horse had no white markings anywhere on his body. He looked like he could have stood to lose a few pounds. The arch of his rump and the crest of his neck were a little too fleshy for his own good. He had decent conformation with nice solid feet that had been well cared for. All in all he was a very cute little guy, although he really didn't have any distinguishable features. And unless you watched him for a few moments and saw him taking cautious steps, or you looked closely at his eyes, you wouldn't know anything was wrong. But the little bay gelding was completely blind.

He had been born on a farm located about two hours south of us. The family raised cattle and bred Morgan horses. In the spring of 2000 their top brood mare gave birth prematurely to a bay colt. His frame was smaller than the other babies on the farm, and he was slightly underweight, but other than that he appeared to be in good health. The family suspected nothing wrong.

When the colt was only a few weeks old, just about the age when babies will start to leave their dam's side and do a tiny bit of exploring on their own, the family noticed that he was running into things. An examination by a veterinarian would reveal extensive scar tissue and clouding over both eyes, rendering him blind.

The owners had the little colt gelded and allowed him to grow up beside his dam till he was close to a year old, at which time they weaned him and then placed him in a small paddock by himself. He was never turned out with the other horses on their farm for fear he would be injured. He learned his fence lines and knew where the water trough was located. The children paid attention to him, giving him treats and brushing his coat, but the horse was clearly unhappy. He did not do well in isolation, for no horse does, and he spent his time pacing back and forth, calling out to the other horses that he could hear and smell in the nearby pastures.

When the horse was nearly six years old, the patriarch of the family had finally had enough. He saw no reason to continue feeding a horse they would never be able to use or sell. And the horse was miserable. The father made the decision to have him put down. But a teenage daughter wailed in protest and begged him to give her time to find an alternative. She eventually found Proud Spirit. When she and I spoke on the phone she told me how her father insisted it was foolish not to put the horse down.

"I just don't see the sense in him standing around, all by himself, and being miserable," he told me when he came to the phone.

"Well, I agree with you," I said. "But I believe he can be turned out and be with other horses."

"He'll get hurt," the father flatly stated.

"Horses have remarkable awareness of their surroundings," I said.

"If they can see," he said.

"Way beyond sight," I told him. "If the fencing is safe, and the pasture is free from debris and he has a few good buddies, I believe he'll be just fine."

He refused to deal with this at his own farm and finally agreed to let us give him a chance at Proud Spirit.

The teenage daughter I had spoken to on the phone met me and Jim in the driveway the day we came for the horse. There were three younger daughters standing over by a small paddock where the little gelding was being kept. They were all crying over the horse's departure.

I felt bad for them and didn't understand why their father insisted on getting rid of the horse, especially if his daughters loved him so. Or even why he had isolated the horse from the others. I noticed that the farm had several pastures which were small enough and safe enough for the blind horse to be able to navigate and learn the terrain. And there were horses in each one so he would have companionship. There was simply no reason not to turn the blind horse out with the others. And there was really no reason why he couldn't even be ridden. But I said nothing.

We let the girls say good-bye, and then walked the horse to the trailer. He never mistook a step. We were handed some paperwork from the father and were on our way.

Just a few minutes into the two-hour ride home back to Proud Spirit I looked over at Jim. "Think we oughta change his name?" I asked. I was kidding, of course. We would absolutely change his name.

"What the heck were they calling him?" Jim said.

"Stumbles," I replied, shaking my head. The name struck me

as sad and we both thought it was awful. But for some reason we both burst out laughing at the absurdity of it. We gave some thought to a new name on the ride home and settled on calling him Joe.

Unfortunately, I hadn't given any thought to where I would put him once we arrived. My instincts with horses have always been that we get in their way too much. We think we have to protect them from themselves and interfere with the instinctual way they work things out. I try to make decisions regarding their health and well-being based on their natural environment.

Whenever we bring a new horse to the sanctuary, providing they are sound enough to function in a herd, we turn them out immediately. Oftentimes they are literally led off the trailer and taken directly to the pasture and simply turned free to go meet the forty-plus horses waiting there. Since the beginning of Proud Spirit, we've taken in over 150 horses and have never had one get hurt by allowing them this freedom to simply be what they are: horses. But there are seasoned horse people who have been shocked to hear this. I am often asked: "You mean you don't put a new horse in a corral till they get to know the place?" My response is, how can they get to know the place if they're stuck in a corral?

You can pen a new horse up for two days, two weeks, or even two months, while they get to know the place. But they are still going to do what they would have done if you had turned them out within two minutes of arriving.

But Joe was a different matter entirely. The odds would be against a blind horse surviving in the wild. Putting him in our main pasture, 160 acres running forty-plus horses, was completely out of the question. That would be too much terrain for him to get acclimated to and it would be too much for him to deal with all the herd dynamics.

We had the two small paddocks, one near the house and one around the barn. They were built in the event that one of our horses came up sick or injured and needed to be isolated, or if we took in a horse who was physically unable to function in a herd. But I couldn't see putting Joe in one of those. That would be no different than the situation he was in before.

Jim came over and let Joe sniff his arm, and then he reached up to rub the horse's neck. "He sure is calm," Jim said.

I nodded in agreement. "He really is a terrific little guy." I looked past Jim and Joe, out to the ten-acre pasture behind the barn. We currently had four horses there: three elderly geldings and one older mare. "I'm thinking back there," I said.

Jim glanced in the direction I was looking. "That should be fine. There's really no other choice."

"But what about the trouble we have with Sophie?" My eyes were squinted in thought and I was still unsure about what to do.

• • •

Sophie had come to us when she was twenty-two years old. She had spent her entire life being bred over and over, having baby after baby. When her owners no longer wanted to breed her, she was put out to pasture and used as a babysitter to scores of weanlings that had just been taken from their dams. When Sophie first arrived at Proud Spirit we placed her out front, in the big main pasture. She was in decent shape for an old gal and could easily hold her own in the large herd.

Our six babies, Riley, Cocoa, Tuxedo, Jackson, Dixie, and Ruby were all just about one year old, and for some reason they all gravitated to Sophie. But she would have none of it. When any one of them came close to her, she wheeled around like a tornado and blasted out with a swift kick. She didn't squeal out in irritation or pin her ears and give them a chance to get out of her space. She didn't even move backwards telling them they better get along. She just clobbered them with no warning at all.

Sophie's determination to keep the babies at a distance escalated into a disturbing situation. She began going after them from twenty or thirty feet away. One of them would be simply grazing, essentially nowhere near her. Sophie would lunge into a full gallop with her teeth bared and slash the hide of the unsuspecting yearling. Things began to worsen when several of the adult geldings began challenging her. And then they started going after her with a vengeance. It was as though they sensed her disruptive behavior and were trying to run her off, while she spent all her time trying to keep everyone away.

It was time to intervene and restore harmony to the herd. We decided to move Sophie into the smaller pasture we had set up for the older horses. There were three elderly geldings already pastured there—Phoenix, Dually, and my boy, Strut. When I moved Sophie in with them, the old guys weren't in the least bit interested in her and she couldn't have cared less about them. Peace had once again been restored to Proud Spirit.

But what about Joe? How would he fit in? I wasn't concerned about the geldings. It was Sophie. My biggest fear was that he would come to stand beside her, or come any where near her for that matter, and she would not tolerate it. But he wouldn't see a kick or a vicious bite coming. He wouldn't know to get out of they way till after the fact. If Sophie chose to, she could make his life a living torment. He would never know where to turn or where to stand.

I expressed my worries to Jim. "All we can do is give it a try," he said. "If she causes problems for him, she'll have to go back out front."

I nodded in agreement. We were resolved with the decision and I turned Joe to walk him back to the pasture. He was a remarkably calm horse. He could feel the tiniest direction from the lead rope and stayed perfectly by my side. We came to stand in front of the gate and I waited for just a moment. The three geldings had watched our approach, but remained where they were. Sophie was off in the distance and never even looked up. I opened the latched gate and led Joe through.

"Take it easy till you find your landmarks, Joey," I said. I reached up to remove the halter. I gave his neck a gentle rub.

"And stay away from that crabby mare," I whispered and sent him on his way.

I recalled a story that had been circulating around the Internet. It had been sent to me numerous times. It told the tale of a blind horse. His owner had put a bell on the halter of another horse so the blind one would always know where his companion was. It was a heartwarming story, but in reality, very silly. A blind horse does not need a bell to know where his herd mates are. And I would imagine it would be irritating to the poor horse who had to wear it.

Joe looked happy to have the halter off and to be moving around on his own. His steps were cautious, but he went off to explore. All three geldings immediately made their way over to say hello. Joe could hear their gentle approach and stood still as he eagerly sniffed the air. The introductions between the four horses were uneventful. The old guys each took a turn smelling the newcomer, who in turn appeared to understand that he had been accepted. Joe was alert, but very relaxed, and he looked so happy to have another horse touching him. He listened to their footfalls and their tails swishing as they turned away and he easily followed them to go off and graze beside them. It was wonderful to see.

I remained at the gate, waiting and watching. Joe hadn't had a drink since the trailer ride. But he could smell the water in his new pasture and I watched as he made his way over to the large trough. His steps were once again slow and cautious. He came within a few feet of the trough and inched forward till his knees bumped into the big tub. He slowly lowered his head till the whiskers on his muzzle touched the water. I smiled at how incredibly well he was doing as he drank deeply.

Once his thirst was quenched he turned back in the direction of the open pasture. He lifted his head high and I could see him slightly turn one way and then the other as he sniffed the air and listened for the others.

The geldings were about fifty feet away, making all the wonderful noises that horses make; their tails were swishing and they were stomping flies off their legs and blowing little bursts of air to clear their nostrils. Joe easily made his way over to them and simply started grazing along side. I was thrilled for him!

But I still wasn't going to leave till I saw how Sophie would behave. She still had not even looked up. This was typical of her disinterest in other horses. But eventually, she and Joe would come within close proximity of each other. It happened sooner rather than later. Something about the little bay horse finally caught her attention. She began walking over to where he was grazing with the geldings.

I was quite surprised she was even interested in Joe. I was also a little nervous about what would happen. But I had to chuckle in spite of myself. As though it had been rehearsed, the three old guys noticed Sophie approaching and they smartly moved away. Apparently there was no longer any need for "conversation" between Sophie and the geldings about who was alpha.

Poor, unsuspecting Joe lifted his head high in the air while his nostrils twitched for a scent. He could hear a horse whom he had not yet met coming from one side, while on the other side his three new buddies moved away. He kept his feet right where they were as he turned his head in Sophie's direction.

I gripped the halter in my hand just a little tighter and found myself leaning forward. "Be nice," I whispered.

Sophie came within a foot or two of where Joe stood and put her head down. Joe could sense or smell where her muzzle was and put his own head down, directly against Sophie's. They said hello, breathing in each other's breath. They both pulled back, just slightly, then found each other's mouths again and resumed saying hello. And then the little blind gelding stepped forward and put his chest against Sophie's shoulder. I clenched my teeth in anticipation of her reaction. But it was suddenly clear that nothing bad was going to happen.

She did not protest when he moved her back a few steps. He finally rubbed his face down the side of her neck and nipped at the top of her mane. I was ecstatic. I had been waiting for a high-pitched squeal of irritation, followed by a whirling body and a well-placed kick. But Sophie was completely accepting.

Joe stepped backwards and brought his face back up to Sophie's. He found the side of her muzzle and gave her a little nip, popping his lips against the side of her mouth. Sophie did squeal, but it was more flirtatious.

This was amazing. Sophie had been turned out with forty-plus horses in our main pasture for several months and she wouldn't let a single one of them into her space. She had spent an entire year with Phoenix, Dually, and Strut and she just barely tolerated all three of them—and that was because they knew not to challenge her and had no interest in a confrontation. But why, out of all these horses, did Sophie choose to accept Joe and help him acclimate to his new home? To say she understood his blindness and mustered some compassion for him is an anthropomorphism that would make practical people cringe. Perhaps there are things that we humans will never understand. I really can't explain these extraordinary events that happen between our horses. I'm just thankful that I'm a witness to it all and allowed to be a part of their lives.

It has been over a year since Joe arrived. In all this time Sophie has never expressed one moment of unkindness towards him. And Joe is doing fantastically. He knows every inch of his ten-acre pasture and has never been hurt, either by the environment or the other horses. He knows his fence lines and where all the trees are. We've even seen him running. What a joy that was! And I'm so very, very grateful that we were able to give him this life of freedom. This life he deserves.

Indigo and the Mustangs

"WELL, HELLO THERE," I SAID TO THE MUSTANG who had just walked into our garage. I turned my head ever so slightly to smile at him, but I quickly averted my eyes and resumed my chores, as though this were an everyday occurrence. I was in the small laundry room that was adjacent to the garage. My back was to the door as I sorted dirty clothes for another load of washing when I heard him step onto the concrete.

His name was Indigo. He had only been with us for a little over one week and had, thus far, found no compelling reason to interact with us or seek out our company. In fact, he vigorously avoided us, walking to the farthest point in the yard whenever he saw anyone come out of the house. We were using the front lawn as his paddock while he recovered from major surgery. The last time I had checked on him, just a few minutes before, he had been grazing in the shade of two oak trees.

I was a little startled when I first heard his tentative steps on the concrete floor. But now he was staring right at me, standing

Indigo's return to freedom

just twenty feet away. He remained where he was after I had said "hello" to him. I just smiled and turned away, and then I heard him moving closer to the little room where I stood. The ambling *clomp, clomp, clomp* of his hooves broadened my smile.

When he put his head right in the door to watch what I was doing, I had butterflies of happiness in my stomach, but continued to act like this was no big deal. But it was a big deal, for this was the first time that he had come to me. All of our encounters since he arrived at Proud Spirit had been me approaching him. This switch was tremendously significant and I was smiling with joy as I continued to separate clothes.

"I don't know, Indigo," I sighed dramatically as I straightened from my task. "I'd say you're pretty domesticated now, doing laundry and all." He didn't respond, but stayed right where he

194

was and continued to watch me. "Wild horse, indeed," I added with mock sarcasm as I lifted the lid of the washer. I was careful to tone down my movements so as not to startle him.

I stood very still for another moment, not facing him, and then I eased my left arm around to the small of my back and extended my hand in his direction. I could feel his warm breath on my skin as he leaned closer to investigate my waggling fingers. Finally, he came close enough for me to feel the whiskers on his muzzle and I remained perfectly still, even holding my breath. He touched my hand with his velvet nose and gave me a tiny nudge. I wanted to whirl around and hug his neck, but I didn't.

"That's right," I breathed out. "You're safe now."

I put my head down and turned slightly so he could see my eyes. The dun-colored Mustang took one step back as he watched me pivot, but he did not retreat. He was less than a foot away. His wonderful horse smell filled my nostrils. We stared at each other and I could see my own reflection in his liquid brown eyes.

"You'll never hurt again," I whispered through my beaming smile.

• • •

Just a little over a year before, Indigo, the Mustang standing in my garage, had been an eight-year-old wild stallion, living with a band of mares in the Steens Mountains near Burns, Oregon. He was one of hundreds of horses captured in a round-up orchestrated by the Bureau of Land Management (BLM) as part of a cull to reduce the numbers of free roaming horses on public lands.

It seems that whenever man gets his hands involved in anything, even when he thinks he's doing good, some sort of problems usually arise. This creates controversy and then naturally people take sides. The horse world is no different.

Many people would agree that there are five major issues in the equestrian community that spark the most heated debate.

They are the Thoroughbred racing industry, Tennessee Walking Horse show industry, Pregnant Mare Urine farms, the slaughter industry, and the BLM's management of America's free-roaming wild horses. These are all controversial, emotionally charged issues, and just about everyone who loves horses has an opinion. But to me, the latter, the issue of America's wild horses, is more complex than any of the others.

For instance, the Thoroughbred racing industry is controversial, but it isn't very complex. Anyone with even a rudimentary understanding of the equine skeletal structure could tell you that you can't run two-year-olds as hard as the Thoroughbred racing industry runs them. No one can defend it. No vet, no trainer, no breeder, no owner. There's only one reason they do it: greed and money. If this were not the case, they'd wait till the horses are older and their bones have matured.

Recently in the spotlight was the young colt Barbaro. In his bid for the Triple Crown his back leg shattered and he would eventually be euthanized. Right after this tragedy happened I read the articles and listened as reporters interviewed everyone in Barbaro's camp. His trainers, the vets, even his owners—they all kept repeating the same sentence over and over in nearly every interview: "Just one bad step," they said as they sadly shook their head over the colt's broken leg that horrible day in May of 2006. But what actually happened was grossly downplayed to define it as a "just one bad step," and I listened to the interviews wishing one of them had the courage to acknowledge that these horses are just babies and they simply should not be run this young.

In the August 2007 issue of *Vanity Fair*, columnist Buzz Bissinger writes about how Barbaro was "betrayed by his own Thoroughbred body." He wasn't betrayed by his own body, he was betrayed by everyone around him. He was just a baby. And he, and every Thoroughbred like him, was being pushed like seasoned adult athletes when their bones and joints haven't fully developed. They cannot physically hold up under the intense stress. The result is the heartbreaking fate which Barbaro suffered.

Unfortunately, there are thousands like him every season. We just don't hear about them because so few are Triple Crown contenders, the injuries don't happen in the spotlight of the Preakness, and there are no heroic efforts to save them. Barbaro had the pure heart and the extraordinary greatness to win if only they had allowed him to mature and strengthen.

As far as the other issues—the Tennessee Walking Horse show industry and its barbaric act of "soring," or blistering a horse's legs to give it a distinctive gait; PMU farms keeping thousands of mares in horrific conditions and sending their foals to slaughter; and the very existence of slaughter in and of itself—it's not very complex to decipher the wrong in all of these.

But what about America's wild horses and how they're being managed? In the nineteenth century more than two million wild horses roamed the American West. By 2002 the Bureau of Land Management estimated that approximately fifty thousand were all that remained. At the time of this writing there are fewer than twenty-five thousand roaming free.

Understanding the complexity of this issue requires one to look back at our own history, the implementation of regulation programs, the mandate of public grazing lands, compassion toward the horses, the environment, water rights, input from the public, and group involvement. Ranchers and other special interest groups want the numbers of wild horses decreased even more than they are. Some want them eliminated completely from public grazing land.

Numerous wild horse preservation groups want them left completely alone, while other rescue organizations advocate minor intervention to control populations. But even the groups who advocate controlling population levels start fighting among themselves about *how* to control it. There are some who are not opposed to the round-ups, but object to the way they are carried out, citing the fact that a number of horses suffer injury as they are chased by helicopters, others die, and foals are often separated from their dams. Others say it's a necessary evil. Some individual western states want control of their own herd management areas. But regulators contend that this is unreasonable as horses in the wild are migratory and cross in and out of state boundaries.

The BLM, who manages these herds, must operate under specific funding appropriated by Congress and at the behest of ranchers they are rounding up horses by the hundreds. Thousands are being held in long-term holding facilities at the expense of the taxpayers. All these different factions are fighting with each other. Then add in the environmental issues: water shortages, trying to preserve delicate native plants, maintaining forage for native animals, and preservation of public grazing lands. It's almost impossible to maintain a harmonious balance.

Media attention has prompted a surge among rescue groups to save these horses, and as a result adoptions of wild Mustangs are increasing. Unfortunately, this has created an entirely new set of problems for this majestic symbol of America's heritage. Inexperienced people are bringing home previously unhandled adult wild horses and they don't have the first clue about how to handle them. It is a dangerous and disheartening situation for both horse and human.

Our focus at Proud Spirit has primarily been on domestic horses. But we have recently had a sobering influx of requests from various people around the country asking us to take in a wild horse they adopted after they found the horse was too much for them to handle. The names and places are different, but the stories are often the same. After three months or more, sometimes longer—even up to a year—people have contacted us because they were as yet unable to even touch the horse, let alone begin working on training them. The horse was, essentially, still wild.

Before taking on a wild horse it is imperative to educate yourself or hire a reputable *experienced* trainer who understands wild horses and will work with them in a kind and humane manner.

People usually make one of two mistakes when trying to domesticate a horse from the wild. They are either too rough or they're too soft. We have dealt with the end results of both of these misguided tactics when we've taken in one of these horses at Proud Spirit, and believe that neither one yields positive results.

There is an essential balance of being fair while providing leadership. And that does not mean "showing the horse who's boss." After all, your ultimate goal is to have a willing partner. What it does mean is having the finesse and experience to tap into what motivates a prey animal ingrained with a thousand years of survival instinct dictating its every move.

But something we need to understand is that this goes beyond what even a good equestrian might acknowledge about these natural instincts. There's a fundamental difference between horses born into domestication and horses born in the wild. For example, horses possess both binocular and monocular vision. This means that, like us, they can focus in on one object, but they can also process separate pictures with each eye at the same time. What some people don't realize is that this "eye transfer" generally doesn't develop as acutely in domestic horses as it does in horses born in the wild simply because it doesn't have to.

We have taken in numerous domestic horses deemed difficult by their previous owner. When I am working on gentling these horses, I usually remain quiet, relying on my body language to communicate with them. We have also taken in several previously unhandled wild horses. When I am working with them, I'm talking all the time. The difference is that a wild horse must become acclimated to the sound of the human voice. This is something many people don't think about.

Likewise, it's the same in helping them acclimate with every single aspect of all their senses, all their fight-or-flight instincts. Imagine the most high-headed, alert, or wary domestic horse you know. Now multiply that by ten. That's what you're dealing with when you bring a previously unhandled adult horse out of the wild. Every movement, every sound, every smell associated with humans, your farm, and everything you accept as part of the landscape is potentially life-threatening to them and cause for a heightened alert—tenfold what it is for a horse born into domestication. I know seasoned horsemen who don't, or won't, understand this.

To get these horses to trust, for them to become willing partners, takes immeasurable patience and a strong commitment to educating yourself above and beyond all your notions and preconceived conceptions about horses and how to gentle them.

One afternoon I received a phone call from two very close friends of mine, Caryn and Tory. They live in a small town a few miles south of Savannah, Georgia. I met them at an equestrian seminar we were all attending in 2000. We became good friends during that weekend and have remained close. Caryn called to tell me that she had been driving down a back road near her home when she noticed a purebred Kiger Mustang standing in a bare dirt paddock. This is the same breed of horse that was the subject of the DreamWorks animation film *Spirit: Stallion of the Cimarron.*

Sadly, the horse in the sandlot did not even begin to resemble the glorious creature depicted in the cartoon. The horse in the sand lot was at least two hundred pounds underweight. He had patches of raw hide where flies and gnats were tormenting him. He appeared to be having difficulty breathing. His sides labored to adequately fill his lungs and with every breath he took, his ribs showed through the skin. His dun-colored coat was dull and his long black mane and thick tail were a mass of knots and tangles. The poor horse stood sullen and depressed with his head hanging low.

When Caryn came upon the horse, she was shocked by his appearance. She paused at the fence line for just a moment, and then drove on by and went directly over to Tory's house to tell her about the horse and discuss how they might intervene. Caryn has a deep and genuine compassion for all animals and Tory has extensive experience with wild horses. Together they were involved in advocacy issues and understood the controversial future facing America's wild horses.

They quickly made the decision to jump in Tory's truck and drive back to where the pitiful Mustang lived. As they approached the property, they could see the distinctive BLM brand along the horse's neck. When they pulled into the driveway, a middle-aged woman opened the front door. Caryn and Tory went to introduce themselves. They were not accusing or confrontational about the condition of the horse, but instead talked about Tory's experience with wild Mustangs, and then they politely offered to help.

The woman appeared almost relieved as she listened to what Caryn and Tory told her about their experience with wild horses. The woman explained that she had indeed adopted the horse from the BLM. And then her eyes filled with tears as she spoke of all the romance she envisioned with owning a wild Mustang. But her dream quickly turned into a nightmare. Although she had ridden horses all her life, and considered herself an experienced horsewoman, she did not know how to work with a wild horse and the situation quickly deteriorated.

The horse she adopted was ten years old and had never seen a human being until he had been rounded up in one of the BLM's culls.

Like all of these displaced horses, everything about the harsh holding pens terrified him. The horses are never worked with or handled prior to being adopted. They are completely wild. Their pictures are put up on the BLM website, hundreds of them, and some are eventually adopted. To move them to their new homes, they are run through shoots and prodded onto stock trailers. This particular horse, the one Caryn and Tory were now trying to save, had been brought from the higher elevation and colder climate of his natural environment of the Steens Mountain Range in Oregon, hauled for five days, and then deposited into the sweltering heat of a south Georgia summer. Unused to the suffocating humidity, he developed respiratory problems and skin infections.

Caryn, Tory, and the horse's owner were standing near the paddock where he was being kept. He was sick, depressed, thin, and miserable.

"I can't even tend to that skin problem," the woman said. "I can't believe the mess I've gotten into." Caryn immediately thought to herself: I can't believe the mess this poor horse is in.

The woman had had him for over a year, and he'd never felt the touch of a human hand; no one could get near him. She told Caryn and Tory that her brother-in-law finally stepped in to help a few weeks ago. He threw a rope around the horse's neck, and then snub tied him to a post where they let him fight the restraints without water for twenty-four hours. They accomplished two things: the Mustang suffered a back injury as he fought the ropes and whatever chance there was for a compatible relationship had been destroyed. The horse tried to bite the brother-in-law when he went to remove the ropes, and now the woman was terrified to go near him, to the extent that she was barely feeding him.

"What now?" I asked Caryn the day she and Tory phoned. "What's going to happen to him?" I was deeply saddened and troubled listening to what this horse had been through.

"Good news," Caryn said. "We've already moved him to Tory's. The woman gave him to us."

"Wow, you guys are amazing," I said. "That's great that she let him go. What a tragedy he's been through. So how is he?"

"He's wild, that's for sure," Caryn told me. "But he actually seems very interested in us and has already calmed down nicely. Tory has him in one of her big, open-air stalls, so he's finally out of the sun. We're pretty much just leaving him alone right now so he can rest, and he's eating his hay and drinking very well."

"What are your plans for him?" I asked.

"Well—" she said slowly. "That's why I'm calling you."

"Ah ha." I smiled.

"Yeah," Caryn said, chuckling. "Um . . . Tory and I have talked about it at length. We think this boy needs Proud Spirit.

We have fallen madly in love with him and we are heartbroken over the hell he's been through. I've never seen a horse so depressed. It's unbearable. We can't stand the thought of trying to adopt him out, even though we'd assure it would be to someone who knew what they were doing and would never hurt him." She paused for just a second. I could hear the emotion building in her voice. "Oh, Mel, we just can't stand the thought of him being trained and saddled. He deserves to be what he is. He deserves to be free."

I smiled, proud to call Tory and Caryn my friends. Not every horse has to be in service to man. They all don't "need a job," and very few people recognize this. Sometimes, enough is enough, and they just need to be left alone. "If you can figure out how to get him here, I'll take him," I said.

They named the Mustang Indigo and immediately found a professional hauler who was willing to deal with a wild horse. Indigo was on his way to Proud Spirit within a few weeks of being relinquished by the woman who adopted him.

I anxiously awaited his arrival. The day after the hauler left Georgia, I received a phone call from him shortly after noon. I thought he was just calling to check in and give me his ETA. But that was not the case. "I've got bad news about this Mustang we're bringing you," he said.

"What's wrong?"

"He's gone down in the trailer," he told me. "I think he's colicking. And it's bad."

"Oh, no," I breathed out. "Where are you?"

"I'm in Missouri, just outside of Columbia. We had to make some other stops up this way before we circled back down to you."

"Can you find a vet?" I asked. My heart was racing. I couldn't believe what this poor horse was going through, after everything he had already endured.

"Well, I already looked on a map. I'm only twenty miles from the University of Missouri and that big equine hospital there.

What do you want me to do?"

"Go," I said. "Get him there."

Less than an hour later my phone rang again. I had been pacing nearby and snatched it from the charger. It was the attending veterinarian from the University of Missouri equine hospital. "You're going to have to make an immediate decision," he told me after we had introduced ourselves. "This horse has a life-threatening impaction. We need to do emergency surgery, right now, or put him down. He's in tremendous pain."

I realized that I'd been holding my breath. I let the air out of my lungs. I knew what my decision would be, but my mind raced through the doubts. My first thought was that I had never even laid eyes on this horse. My second thought was the money. Colic surgery could cost over five thousand dollars. The bill could be even higher if there were complications. Where would we get the money?

"I need three minutes," I told the vet. "Give me a moment to think about this and I will call you back in three minutes." We hung up and I called Tory's cell phone. I quickly explained what was happening. "What do we do?" I said.

"Mel, no horse should survive the hell this horse has been through only to die on the way to Proud Spirit, on the way to getting his life back," she said. "Don't let him die."

I quickly called the hospital back and the veterinarian answered on the first ring. "Do the surgery," I said. I knew in my heart what my decision would be before I even called Tory. But I needed her to be involved.

Indigo had successful colic surgery. A deadly impaction of sand had been removed from his intestines. He would spend two weeks recovering at the University of Missouri equine hospital. The attending veterinarians phoned with frequent updates and I was impressed not only with the professionalism of the entire staff, but also how kind and friendly they all were. They explained everything that transpired throughout Indigo's stay with them and never rushed my questions.

We were advised that Indigo would have to remain stalled for an additional two weeks after he arrived at Proud Spirit. So while he was still in the hospital we quickly built a large, free-standing stall right out in the front yard. I didn't want him isolated down in the barn once we brought him home. I wanted him near the house so he could see us all day long and get used to hearing our voices.

Indigo had finally recovered enough to complete his journey to our sanctuary. I enlisted my friend Paul to make the trip up to Missouri and bring Indigo safely home. He was an experienced horseman and if a problem arose I was confident that Paul would be able to handle it.

The day Paul delivered Indigo to Proud Spirit was very emotional. Paul led him off the trailer and handed me his lead rope. I felt that this horse and I already had a history, but it was the first time we had actually looked at each other.

"Hey, there," I said quietly. I reached up to touch his neck. I could see the patch of shaved hair where the IV needle had been. His entire stomach was shaved as well. He still had a period of recovery, but I felt in my heart that his troubles were over.

I used the time that he had to remain stalled as an opportunity to develop a very close bond with him. Tory had handled him slightly during the short time he was at her house, and he was handled extensively by the staff at the equine hospital, but he was still wary of humans and would not allow me to touch him unless he was corralled in his stall. I needed to further gentle him to the extent that he would accept a level of tameness. We would never break him to ride; he would never have a saddle on his back or feel a bit in his mouth. But he had to accept our touch.

Within a very short time I could put my hands anywhere on his body and easily tend to the eight-inch incision on his stomach. I also used the opportunity to soothe him with TTouch™, a method of hands-on therapy developed by Linda Tellington-Jones. I use this extensively on all our horses and consider it a marvelous way to bond with a new horse while at the same time helping them to relax. I especially love making the gentle circles on their face and around their eyes. The moment when horses accept being touched is clear, as they lower their heads and slowly blink with half-closed lids and then begin to work their mouths and lick their lips.

A few days after Indigo had arrived at Proud Spirit I went out to his big, free-standing stall to say good morning to him and bring him his breakfast. The stall was 12 x 24. At this point he was still moving as far away from me as the walls would permit. I would spend a little time every day getting him used to a halter being put over his head. I would leave it on while I fed him and cleaned his stall, and then I would take it back off. This morning I put the halter on and remained by his side.

I stood quietly for a few moments and then reached up to run my fingers through his black mane. It hung down below his neck. He was truly beautiful. His coat was a rich dun color, like caramel. He had a dark dorsal stripe that ran along the center of his back. And there were distinctive zebra stripes on the backs of his legs, indicative of the Kiger breed.

I worked my hand up his neck and my fingers ran along his powerful jaw. He shifted his eyes in my direction and I could see the worry and concern over my touch.

"It's okay, pal," I whispered, but didn't remove my hand. I began making gentle circles with the tips of my fingers. Not brushing over the hair, but rather moving the skin. I worked my way up towards his left eye. I found the pronounced vein that runs down a horse's face near the ridge of the nose. I made the small circles along its path and noticed Indigo begin to relax. His eyes had been wide open as he watched me and wondered what I was doing. But suddenly his lids softened.

I stepped closer to him so my back was against his chest and I continued to make the circles along his face. I brought my hand down to his mouth and gently worked the corner of his lips. He brought his head down and nearly closed his eyes.

"That's right," I said quietly. "Nobody's gonna hurt you." He kept his head down in a relaxed position, but opened his eyes at the sound of my voice and I could see him shift his gaze to me. Our faces were just inches apart. I closed my own eyes and leaned my face against his. "You're safe now."

Near the end of his two weeks of stall rest I began letting Indigo out several hours a day to wander around the yard and graze. The afternoon I was sorting clothes in our small laundry room and suddenly heard his footsteps on the concrete will remain with me forever.

This remarkable, beautiful boy, once wild and free, had been dealt an absurd disservice. From the terrifying round-up by the BLM, to the abuse and neglect in captivity, every encounter with man had taken his life from bad to worse. But if this was to be his fate, to become domesticated, we were presented with an extraordinary opportunity to make things right and give this horse the life he deserved.

It was a breathtaking sight the day we turned him loose onto the 320 acres of rolling hills where he could finally join his new herd . . . and live his life in freedom.

The Gift

JOHN BOSSE WAS ONE OF OUR CO-WORKERS from the days when Jim and I were working at the fire department. He was also a fellow horse-lover. He and I spent hours talking about them whenever we were stationed together. John and his wife, Sheri, were both genuine animal lovers. They had a home on five acres where they lived with their two trail horses, Dally and Durango. Their time away from work was spent enjoying each other, their home in the country, and their dogs and horses.

Just months after Jim and I were settled at our new ranch in Arkansas, we received word that Sheri had passed away. We were aware that she had been struggling with illness in the previous months, but there was hope that she was going to recover. Sadly, it was not to be. I was heartbroken for John and knew that he would be devastated. Sheri was only in her forties, much too young. She and John had a deeply committed marriage and were very much in love. More than anything, they were best friends. I immediately sent him a note, telling him how sorry I was and that I would keep him in my thoughts.

John was heavily on my mind over the next few days. One afternoon when the phone rang, just about a week after I had sent him the note, I was surprised to see his name on our caller ID. We were friends and had a lot in common, and I cared very much about John, but our relationship was more along the lines of co-workers. I imagined him turning to others, to whom he was closer, during this difficult time. I wondered what had prompted him to call.

"John," I said. "How are you?"

"Well," he said. His voice quavered and he let out a small little laugh. "Not so good."

We talked for a short time about how he was coping. He cried openly when he expressed the pain of losing his soulmate, and then he told me why he was calling. He wanted to share something that happened in Sheri's final days.

"Once it became clear that she was not going to recover," John began, "the doctors let her come home. Of course, she was bedridden at that point. But she wanted to be able to watch the horses grazing, so I went out and bought one of those futons. I turned the screened-in porch into an outdoor bedroom for her."

I smiled through my tears, but remained quiet. I envisioned wanting the very same thing in my final days that Sheri wanted in hers—to be able to watch my horses. The lump in my throat grew as I tried to imagine how impossibly hard all of this must have been. I didn't trust myself to speak, but I'm sure John heard me sniffling and knew that I was listening.

"One evening we were sitting together," John continued through tears of his own, "watching an incredible sunset. The horses were up close to the house. We could actually hear them munching on the grass. Sheri began talking about what she wanted me to do with various belongings, who she wanted me to give certain things to." He paused for just a moment to compose himself. "We started talking about the horses. Sheri told me that she wanted them to go to you, Mel. She wants them to live out their lives at Proud Spirit."

Without hesitation I told John we would take them. I was deeply touched that Sheri entrusted me with Dally and Durango. John was relieved and felt this would be a powerful step in allowing him to work towards healing, knowing that Sheri's beloved horses would be taken care of for the rest of their lives.

"I just have one other question," John said. "Is there any way that Jim could haul them? I hate to ask, but I'm a little overwhelmed and don't know how I'd get them out there to you."

"We would be more than happy to do that for you, John, but unfortunately we don't have a trailer," I said.

John was surprised to hear me say that. "I never realized you didn't have one," he said.

We had been doing rescue work nearly fifteen years, and somehow we had managed all right without one. We relied on friends and family when we needed to haul, and other times we resorted to hiring someone. It seemed that whenever we had extra funds, they were better spent somewhere else, like building shelters, or going directly to the care of the forty-plus horses, rather than buying a trailer.

John said he would look into some different options available for having the horses shipped out to us, and he'd get back with me. We talked for a few more minutes about his plans, and then hung up.

He called back a few days later. "I've decided that I could use a change of scenery," he said. "I'm going to bring them out myself. A friend is going to come with me and help with the driving."

"Great," I said. "It'll be wonderful to see you and I think it will be good for you to see the new facility. When you think about Dally and Durango you'll be able to picture them at their new home."

John agreed and said he was looking forward to the trip. "I guess I'll see you in about a week," he said.

Some weeks later, John arrived at Proud Spirit with the horses. His friend, Alex, was driving the truck, and just as they pulled into the driveway it began to snow. John and I hugged when he got out of the truck and we both started crying.

"Thank you for doing this," he said through his tears. "I can't tell you—"

He didn't finish. I didn't feel like I would be able to talk either. It was all very emotional, so I just shook my head, telling John he didn't need to say anything more.

John introduced me to Alex, who was wiping tears from his eyes as well. "Well," I said. "Let's get the horses unloaded!"

Dally and Durango were excited to see their new home. We walked them off the trailer, removed their halters, and turned them loose in the paddock near the barn. Healthy horses are perfectly adept at keeping warm in thirty-degree weather, but coming from Florida to this colder environment, Dally and Durango would need a little time to adjust to the change in temperature. I wanted them to be able to get out of the wind and have access to the stalls.

I decided I would even put a blanket on Dally as night fell and the temperatures dropped. She was thirty years old and didn't have much of a natural coat. She was also just a little thin, as is typical with elderly horses. Durango was a big, stocky Quarter horse. He was just six years old and could have handled being turned out with the herd. But I would keep them together and give them both plenty of hay that night and make sure they were comfortable.

The three of us stood watching the horses as they sniffed around their new home and nibbled on the sparse winter grass that poked through the light misting of snow. We chatted about the trip and Alex revealed that he did most of the driving. John was exhausted from the emotional upheaval of losing Sheri and slept most of the way out. Alex said he was happy to see John resting. As we talked a little more I would discover just what a remarkable friend Alex was.

After a short time, I suggested we get out of the cold and I turned to go in the house, motioning for John and Alex to follow me.

"Just a second, Mel," John said, stopping me. "There's something I wanted to tell you." I looked back at him and waited for him to go on. "Today is our anniversary," John smiled. Tears welled in his eyes once again.

"Oh, geez," I said. "I'm so—"

He held up his hand to stop me. "We spent our honeymoon in Hot Springs. Traveling these same roads this week to get here to you, to Mena, I found myself on the same highways Sheri and I took all those years ago to get to Hot Springs." He paused and looked up at the sky. "It even snowed that week," he smiled. He held his hands open to catch the drifting flakes in his palms. "Can you believe it? You don't get much snow here, do you?" I smiled and shook my head "no." "But it snowed then, and it's snowing now," he said. "I guess there are probably people that think stuff like this is silly—" He stopped and looked over at the horses. "But I feel like Sheri is with me. She wanted to make sure the horses got here safe and that they're settled." He started to weep. Alex and I did as well. We both stepped forward and put a hand on John's back.

John took a deep breath and held it, and then finally let the air out of his lungs. He gave both Alex and me a quick hug and then stepped away. "Okay, Alex," he said as he walked over to his truck. John opened the passenger side door and reached in to grab an envelope. He walked back to where I stood and handed it to me. I thought it might be the papers and health certificates on Dally and Durango. I would open it later.

"Open it," he said when he saw me not moving to investigate the contents.

I lifted the flap and peered inside. It was a title and registration. I looked up at John with a furrowed brow, my eyes narrowed in question.

A new trailer for Proud Spirit

"It's to the trailer," he said, tipping his head in the direction of the gleaming rig. "I'm giving it to you. Sheri and I are giving it to you."

I looked from John over to the trailer. Alex was already behind the truck unhooking it. It was a brand-new, three-horse, aluminum-slant Sundowner trailer. John and Sheri had just purchased it, just before she became ill. They had used it only two times. I looked back at John, my face frozen in shock.

"Wha—" I breathed out. I looked back over at the trailer. "I'm—I don't know what to say," I sputtered. "John, I don't know what to say."

"Say 'thank you,'" he said, laughing.

What John did was an act of extraordinary generosity and kindness. When you are involved in rescue work, you see some of the worst of mankind. John gave me a gift beyond the amazing trailer parked in my driveway. He reminded me of the true good in people with the selflessness to live beyond themselves and give back to the world around them. John may never know how he significantly changed our lives at Proud Spirit. We always felt we were managing fine without a trailer, and we were, but there was also an underlying level of anxiety over not having a safe and reliable trailer here on the property, ready for use in the event of an emergency. We would never forget this remarkable gift.

The Boys from Guadalupe

PUBLICITY ABOUT THE SANCTUARY AND OUR WORK rescuing horses has always been a double-edged sword. A newspaper or magazine article might inspire someone to send a note of encouragement, something which is always welcome. Or perhaps someone
might even make a monetary contribution to our efforts, a gesture that is deeply appreciated as most of what we do comes out
of our own pockets. But more often than not, the publicity also
prompts too many people to contact us about taking in a horse.

In March of 2005, PBS filmed a documentary about Proud
Spirit. It originally aired in a limited viewing area, regionally on
the west coast of Florida. The following year the special was nom-
inated for an Emmy, and won. Shortly thereafter plans were made
to release the film nationally. Jim and I were excited about the
positive impact this might have on our rescue work and the
awareness it would bring about for horse welfare.

Nearly every morning I woke up to fifteen or twenty e-mail
messages, sometimes even more, from people all across the coun-

Poco and Slick get a drink while Banjo the llama looks on.

try. Many were thanking us for our love of horses and our dedication to the sanctuary, but there were also the inevitable requests for us to take in a horse someone no longer wanted.

I answered every single e-mail. I let people know how appreciative we were that they took the time to write. To others, I explained why we could not take their horse. Proud Spirit is not a retirement facility. Over the years we have taken in some horses simply because they needed to retire, but that's not really why we're here. We are here for abused, neglected, and abandoned horses, or ones who are confiscated by law enforcement and need a home. "Your horse has a home," I wrote. "If only you would make the commitment to provide him with the retirement he deserves." Essentially, I was telling people that they are the ones who used the horse up so they are the ones who should care for the horse now that he is no longer rideable.

Some of the people we turned down wrote back angry letters. "How dare you accuse me of not committing to my horse! That's why I'm trying to find a place where he can live out his life, rather than sending him to slaughter. I can't keep feeding and taking care of a horse we don't ride." *Oh, but someone else can do it for you,* I thought to myself. *Shouldn't he live out his life with you?* It was absurd to me.

This truly is a huge problem in this country. The entire equestrian community must begin to accept the long-term responsibility of horse ownership. People need to think about what they're going to do with a thousand-pound animal when the kids get bored or the horse suffers an injury or becomes arthritic. Barring an untimely fatal injury or illness, every horse is going to get old and eventually become unridable. What are your long-term plans when this happens? Sanctuaries and rescue groups can't handle it all. And sending them off to slaughter is not a solution. We need to think about this before we bring the horse home.

As the PBS special aired across the country we received many letters praising our accomplishments and the exemplary lifestyle we provided for the horses in our care, while others still found fault. We were criticized for never working the horses who come to our sanctuary. "Horses need a job," some people said. That is just ridiculous. Some couldn't understand our policy of never adopting the horses out. Others questioned our feeding program, our farrier, and veterinary routine. It was endless.

One woman even wrote a nasty letter telling me to shut up about the use of Premarin™. I had no business telling women not to use the drug, she said, when I have "no first-hand knowledge of how difficult it is dealing with menopause." I actually didn't recall ever telling anyone not to use the drug; I simply felt that women who are using it should be aware of how the drug is derived, and that there are other options to explore.

In over fifteen years of doing rescue work this was the first time that I had ever felt truly weary of it all. And it was not from the unyielding responsibility of taking care of the fifty-plus horses we now had day in and day out. The horses were, and still are, my strength. I had the energy and love to care for twice as many. I could even handle the occasional letter that criticized our policies or procedures. That wasn't an issue to me. Everyone has an opinion. I simply thanked people for writing and kept my responses brief in the hopes that a big debate did not ensue.

The difficult thing for me, what put a slump in my shoulders and had me shaking my head with weary sadness, was the knowledge that so many Americans don't care about providing their own horses with a well-deserved retirement. They want someone else to do it for them.

But something extraordinary was about to happen that would renew my energy and restore my faith in mankind.

• • •

On Friday, August 10, 2007, there was a message on my answering machine. It was from a woman named Debra Beene. She was employed as an archaeologist for the state of Texas. Debra's office was located in Austin, and she had just received an unusual request from the administrative offices of the Guadalupe Mountains National Park in Texas near the New Mexico border. The person phoning from Carlsbad told Debra that they needed to dig a hole large enough to bury two horses. They were calling to obtain permission from her department before doing any excavating within the national park boundaries.

Debra did her research, and then gave permission for the park service to dig the large burial hole. In her discussions with the administrator Debra learned that the two horses had been service mounts and were presently being stabled at a remote ranger station high up in the mountains. One of the horses was thirty years old and had been "employed" at the park for twenty years. The other had just turned twenty-five. The two horses had been working together for fifteen years carrying rangers and their gear as they patrolled the vast wilderness. But both horses had become too old to handle the workload and the last year had proved to be too much for them. Their caretaker, Gary Carver, had put in a request for two younger horses.

His request was granted. Unfortunately, unbeknownst to

Gary, the paperwork he innocently submitted several months ago became an unintentional death sentence for the two loyal and hardworking horses that he had loved and cared for, and thought of as his own. Just as soon as permission was granted to dig the grave, the administration made an appointment with a local vet to euthanize the two horses.

That evening at home, Debra couldn't stop thinking about the two old geldings. Something didn't sit right, but she couldn't put her finger on what it was. She began to wonder if the horses really needed to be put down. After all their years of service, why weren't they simply allowed to retire? She walked into the living room and flipped on the TV. A show was just starting on PBS. It was called "The Horses of Proud Spirit." Debra was spellbound by the program and sat watching with tears in her eyes. The very next morning she found our phone number and left a message on our answering machine asking me to call her. She explained the entire situation to me when she and I finally spoke on the following Monday.

Debra told me how she had learned about the two horses up in the Guadalupe Mountains, and then the sequence of events at home which put her in front of the TV at the exact moment the PBS special about Proud Spirit was coming on. "I just can't stop thinking about them," Debra said. "And then I knew I had to do something after I saw your show. If they need to be put down, that's one thing. But if the park service is just doing it to tidy things up, that's a little hard to take."

"I completely agree," I said. "How can I help?"

"I was hoping you could speak to someone at the park," she said. "Evaluate the situation and the health of the horses; make sure this really needs to be done. I would do it, but I don't know enough about horses to even know what questions to ask."

I've never shied away from getting involved. And getting involved does not mean being confrontational, tossing about accusations, or creating problems. It means offering your help and working together to find solutions. If no one ever does anything, then nothing ever gets done. "Get me some phone numbers," I said to Debra.

On Tuesday August 14 I spoke with one of the administrators at the Guadalupe Mountains National Park in Carlsbad. He told me he didn't really know very much about what was going on, but he'd have someone who did return my call. Two days later a woman named Lois called. She was very official and spoke in clipped stern sentences after I explained who I was and why I was calling.

"The two horses you are referring to are government property," she replied. "Unusable government property. It is a waste of taxpayer money to maintain something that isn't usable."

"But they aren't things," I said quietly. Lois and I talked for a few more minutes, but she was clearly not going to be convinced that this conversation held any merit.

Next I phoned Gary Carver. Debra had included his phone number in the list she'd given me. He was the ranger who had been caring for the two horses for several years and using them as his mounts when he patrolled remote areas of the park. I wanted to find out what his feelings were about all this, and whether or not he thought the two horses were in bad enough physical shape that euthanasia was warranted. If anyone would know, Gary would.

"No, they don't need to be put down," he told me. Gary and I had an instant rapport, and I liked him immediately. I could hear a touch of anger, or perhaps exasperation about the situation in his voice. As we spoke, I learned that Gary had been trying for several months to convince the administration to allow him to keep the horses. He made every effort to assure the administration that he would take personal responsibility for their care and upkeep.

"And what did they say," I asked.

"They told me that when I put in a request for a new vehicle, and get issued one, I'm not allowed to keep the old one. This is no different."

"Amazing," I muttered.

"Yeah." He let out a small humorless laugh and I could envision him shaking his head.

We talked for several more minutes about the bureaucracy he has had to contend with in trying to save the lives of these two horses. He also admitted that until he received my phone call he had pretty much given up hope, for the administration had already made an appointment with a veterinarian to euthanize them.

I suddenly had a thought. "Do you think that the 'powers that be' would allow them to come to our sanctuary?" I asked.

"You would do that?" he asked. It was the first time I heard any enthusiasm in his voice. "You would take them in?"

"Yeah," I smiled. "Yeah, I would."

"Let me make some calls," Gary said. We hung up and I went out to my truck to grab my atlas. I flipped to the two-page map of the United States. I found the Guadalupe Mountains. My finger traced the roads connecting our sanctuary in Arkansas to the ranger station outside of Carlsbad where Gary and the horses lived. It looked like a long way away. A very long way . . .

I didn't hear back from Gary the day we initially spoke. Or the next day. Then the weekend was upon us and the horses weighed heavily on my mind. I didn't know when the appointment was to have the horses put down. I worried that maybe they had gone through with it. But the following Monday, August 20, my phone rang. It was Lois.

"I received a phone call last week from Ranger Carver," she said. "He tells me that you run a horse sanctuary, and you may be willing to take the two horses at your facility."

"Not 'may be willing' to take them," I said. "We *are* willing to take them. Without hesitation."

"Hmm," she said, but I was unable to interpret the meaning of her response. After a brief pause, she added, "I'll be in touch." Her tone did not leave an opening for me to ask any questions. We said good-bye and hung up. A few hours later my phone rang again. It was Gary. The horses were still alive. The administration was considering placing them in our custody.

"But they need all sorts of information from you," he said. "They want proof that you are who you say you are. And that you are a legitimate sanctuary."

"No problem," I said. "I'll send them whatever they need."

"Even after you do all that, I truly have no idea if they'll agree to it." He spoke the words cautiously as though he were trying to protect my feelings . . . or else his own.

I sent Lois all the information she requested about Proud Spirit. And while we waited for the final decision to be made, I decided to think positively. I put out a group e-mail to an assortment of horse friends. I explained the entire situation and told everyone about the two elderly horses, and that we were trying to get transportation for them from the Guadalupe Mountains National Park in west Texas to Proud Spirit, about a fifteen-hour drive.

It would be impossible for Jim and me to make the trip, at least together. We had too many dogs, too many horses, and the routine was too complex to leave it all on the spur of the moment in just anyone's hands. It had been years since he and I had been on any sort of vacation together. We had Sarah and Stephen nearby now. We relied on them and trusted them completely, but Sarah was eight months pregnant.

The ideal situation would be for a network of friends to break up the trip. Perhaps someone could pick up the horses from Gary and transport them part of the way. They could meet up with someone else who could make another leg of the trip, and so on. I didn't really have the logistics figured out at this point; I just wanted to make contact with other horse people and see what we all came up with. A message came back through my e-mail almost immediately. It was from our friend Ronnie Garcia. He and his wife, Kathleen, live north of Austin. His note was very short. It just said to call him.

I reached him on his cell phone. "I wanted to let you know," he said, "Kathleen and I will go get the horses." He added that they would volunteer their time and the fuel to do what needed to be done. I was speechless. It was incredible to me that someone would step up this way, no questions asked and without hesitation for two horses they had never met when there was nothing in it for them. I had tears in my eyes as I thanked Ronnie for his kindness.

Now we were just waiting to hear what decision the park administration had made. On August 23, Gary called. "It's a go," he said. I could hear the excitement and emotion in his voice. We both laughed with happiness and gave each other verbal pats on the back through the phone line. "There's only one problem," he added. "They want them out of here before the Labor Day weekend."

"Then that's what we'll do," I shrugged. "Let me check on a few things, and I'll call you right back." I hung up with Gary, and immediately phoned Ronnie. I explained the time frame we were working under, and he said they would make arrangements to leave Tuesday, the 28th.

"We're all set, Gary," I said when I called him back. "We can pick them up on Wednesday the twenty-ninth."

"Perfect," Gary said. "Well, I say perfect. But I'll have to confirm that date with Lois. She's out of the office till Monday. I'll call you back after I speak with her then."

Our phone rang bright and early Monday morning, August 27. "Wednesday is fine with Lois," Gary said.

"All right! Friends of ours who live in Austin are going to transport them for us," I continued. "They are all prepared to leave their place on Tuesday and meet up with you on Wednesday."

There was silence on the other end of the line. "Gary?" I said. "What's wrong?"

I heard him sigh. "You aren't gonna believe this. You can't send friends. They won't release the horses to anyone but you. You personally. I just assumed you would be making the trip.

You'll have to sign papers, which they want to witness. And they want to see you, you personally, drive away with them in your trailer."

"That's nuts!" I exclaimed. "What does it matter who picks them up?"

"I couldn't even begin to guess why they're insisting on this," Gary said.

"Are any of these people capable of thinking outside of their bureaucratic boxes? We can't make that drive, Gary. It's at least fifteen hours one way. It'll take us four days. Jim and I can't leave this place and all these animals for that long." My words came tumbling out in knee-jerk reaction. Gary remained quiet.

I finally stopped talking and took a deep breath. I knew that I would make this work and I would simply do what needed to be done. It was Monday. I would need to be on the road by the next day. Jim and I spent the day pondering the best solution: who would go, who would stay, or who would take care of things if we both went. Providing I could find someone to make the drive with me, we decided that Jim would stay home to tend to things here.

Tuesday morning, August 28, I called my friend Charlena. She and her husband, Chris, were friends of ours from Florida. They were both firefighters at the same department where Jim and I worked and we had been friends for years. We were all still in our mid-forties when we were able to retire, and like us, Chris and Char had planned to leave Florida as soon as they were able. Oklahoma had always intrigued them and about a year after we moved, they found a forty-acre ranch near the Arkansas-Oklahoma state line, just an hour away from us.

"Hey! Wanna go on a road trip?" I said when Char picked up the phone.

"When?" she asked.

"Well," I laughed, "just as soon as you can get here."

"What am I packing for, and for how many days?"

"We're going to west Texas to pick up two horses. We'll be gone four days."

She didn't ask anything else. "I'll be there in two hours." *Now that's a good friend,* I thought.

I immediately headed outside to hook up the trailer. As I lined the ball up under the gooseneck hitch I said a silent "thank you" to John Bosse. I was so deeply grateful for his donation of this safe, modern trailer, which would easily haul two large horses in comfort. If it had not been for his kindness and generosity I would not even be making this trip, and we would be scrambling to figure out how to save the lives of the two park service horses who deserved a peaceful retirement at Proud Spirit.

Char arrived in record time. We threw our bags in the back seat of my truck and hit the road. The miles flew by as we traversed the lush rolling terrain of Arkansas and the hill country of central Texas. We spent the night outside of Abilene. But the next morning we hit the flat highways that shoot straight through the desolate landscape of west Texas and time seemed to move backwards. I pulled a few CDs from the center console of my truck and we entertained ourselves by singing along with Don Edwards and his ballads about cowboys, cattle, and coyotes, and Mary Ann Kennedy as she sang her wonderful love stories about her own beloved horses, loyal dogs, and comical barn cats.

We finally made it halfway across our monotonous route when we came to a run-down, tiny town in the middle of nowhere. I pulled alongside the fuel pumps of the one and only convenience store. Char went in to grab us some sandwiches and something to drink while I filled the truck. I hopped out with my charge card in hand and then stood dumbly in front of the ancient pump looking for the slot where I could swipe my Visa. I searched all over as I tipped my head to the left, and then to the right. Finally I stepped back to get a better perspective of the entire front of the pump.

"Where the hell is the slot for the charge card?" I asked myself out loud.

"Don't got one," a voice behind me said. I turned around to see a stout older woman walking in my direction. "I gotta turn it on for ya. Yer the first of the day," she said. Her long gray hair was pulled back into a harsh ponytail. Her face was leather tough and etched with lines from the relentless west Texas sun. She came to the back of my pickup and ducked under the gooseneck of the trailer. I saw her glance down at my license plate. "Arkansas, huh?" she said as she approached the pump with a key in her hand.

"Yes, ma'am," I answered.

She lifted a hand in a dismissive wave. "Oh honey, callin' me ma'am is like hangin' frilly curtains in a outhouse. The two jus' don't gee and haw." I laughed at her analogy, and at her reference to a term old-timers use when two plow mules get along in perfect harmony. She inserted the key she was carrying into the keyhole and pulled a lever. The dial on the pump whirred and zeroed down. "There ya go," she said with a smile. "Better fill all the way up if yer headin' across the flats. There's nothin' b'tween here and there."

You mean it gets worse, I thought to myself. "How much longer is it to Carlsbad?" I asked as I unscrewed my gas cap.

She leaned against my truck and hitched an elbow across the rail of the bed. "It's a far piece," she said, looking west, and said nothing more. I nodded wisely, as though I had a perfect understanding of how far a "far piece" was.

"Where you from in Arkansas?" she asked.

"Mena," I replied, and waited for the inevitable "where's Mena." You never meet anyone who knows where Mena is.

"Mena, huh?" the woman repeated as she pushed away from my truck and stood up straight. "Hey, JD!" she hollered. I looked in the direction she had called. A nice looking man in his late sixties stepped off the porch of the store and started walking in our direction. He was wearing blue jeans and a crisp snap-front cowboy shirt. "This gal is from Mena," the woman told him. He came to my side and stuck out his hand. I took it as I looked into his friendly, smiling eyes and we shook hands.

"Name's JD," he said. "I was born and raised in Mena. You never meet anyone who knows where Mena is, let alone is actually from there." We laughed about the unlikely coincidence and I explained that we had only lived there a few years, but Jim and I loved it as if we'd been there our whole life. Char came out of the store and we all chatted and laughed for over a half-hour. We learned that JD had been in this town since his early twenties and he was the owner of the convenience store. Millie, the woman who turned on the gas pump for me, was his wife. They wanted to know why we were passing through their part of the country. We told them all about the horses and our mission to rescue them. We, in turn, wanted to know what in the world had enticed JD to leave the lush beauty of west central Arkansas for this dilapidated desert town.

An easy smiled crossed his face. "You're not the first one to ask that," he laughed. He turned away slightly, and looked up and down the mostly empty main street with several boarded-up store fronts. The smile was still on his lips as he turned back to face me. "A town is its people," he said. "And to me, this town is the most beautiful place on earth. You'll never find more honest or friendly folks than these." He went on to recount some marvelous stories and I loved hearing about his town and the folks who lived there.

JD and Millie were truly wonderful people, genuine and full of life. I felt uplifted simply for having met them. They both waved until we rounded the corner of the little filling station and were out of sight. And with the sincerity of his words still in my head, I saw a different town than the one we had pulled into just a little over a half-hour before.

We were met in Carlsbad by a park official. He would be escorting us up into the Guadalupe Mountains and the ranger station where the horses were being stabled. Once we arrived, he would witness my signature and watch me load the horses onto my trailer, and then escort us back down. We followed his white, government-issue sedan for two hours. Up we climbed along the twisting, turning, narrow road that cut through thousands of acres of fascinating terrain. There was absolutely no sign of civilization. It was breathtaking when we reached the nearly seven-thousand-foot elevation.

We finally came to the ranger station in the middle of this amazingly diverse wilderness. You could see for miles, the air was so sweet, and the silence was indescribable. Hawks circled lazily overhead as they caught the uprising drafts of air. The flora and the fauna seemed delicate and rugged all at the same time.

There was a small office where campers and hikers could check in. Behind the office was the ranger's living quarters, and a little further up the road stood a barn and some stables. Ranger Gary Carver came out of the house when he heard us pull in. I got out of the truck and went to introduce myself.

"Thank you," he said as we shook hands. He was a tall man with friendly eyes and a capable demeanor. I got the feeling that he did not suffer fools. He was dressed all in khaki, including the hat that shaded his face from the sun. I just smiled at him and nodded in response. "Let's go meet the horses," he added.

From that point on everything began to move too fast. I barely had time to get acquainted with the two geldings, let alone enjoy the spectacular scenery. I wanted some time to spend with Gary so he and I could talk and get to know each other. I wanted to hear stories about his life with these horses. I wanted to simply hear about the horses. But paperwork was spread across the trunk of the white car that had led us up the mountain. A pen was put under my nose and I was shown where to sign. The two horses were haltered and then Gary and I loaded them onto the trailer. Suddenly the sedan door slammed shut and the engine roared to life.

I looked around, feeling a little lost at the way this all transpired, like a big blur. But there was nothing I could do, and so Charlena and I climbed back in my truck. I followed the sedan out of the barn area, but something compelled me to stop near the office and look in my rearview mirror. I put my truck in park, ignoring the white car in front of me, and walked back to where Gary stood. His eyes were glimmering with unshed tears. He was staring at the trailer. I stepped close to him and we just looked at each other. Neither one of us said a word.

I wondered about this man standing before me. Living up here, completely alone, surrounded by thousands of acres of uninhabited land. I felt heartsick for him that these horses, his partners, were being taken away. It was beyond absurd that he wasn't allowed to keep them, and that they weren't allowed to live out their life with the man who loved and cared for them for so many years. I instinctively moved forward to give him a hug. He momentarily returned my embrace and then abruptly set me away from him.

He quickly wiped his eyes and then reached into his shirt pocket and pulled out a card. "Here's my e-mail," he said. I took it from him and looked down at the address. "Don't send me a bunch of long sappy messages," he added. "Just let me know they're okay." I smiled at his gruff exterior and nodded as I wiped my own tears away.

It was almost dark by the time we made it down the mountain and pulled back into Carlsbad. I was a nervous wreck after two hours of pulling a trailer carrying two thousand pounds of horse down the treacherous switchback curves and didn't want to drive any further. We found an equine vet on the outskirts of town who said she would board the horses for us over night at her own house. Her name was Samantha, but she told us to call her Sami. She was a wonderful young woman, just starting a new practice. She helped us unload the horses and put them in one of her paddocks. Once they were settled, Char and I left to find a hotel and eat a meal.

The following morning we met Sami in her driveway. She was preparing to leave on her rounds. "What do I owe you?" I asked, after the horses were loaded back onto the trailer.

"Nothing," she smiled. "This is great what you're doing." We shook hands as I thanked her for her kindness, and then we were ready to get back on the road.

Before we got underway Char pulled out the map and we determined that the halfway point would be somewhere around Stephenville, Texas, "The Cowboy Capital of the World." I didn't want the horses in the trailer for more than eight hours. We felt we could make it to Stephenville in about six, so that's where we planned to spend the night.

I phoned my sister-in-law, Carolyn, and asked her if she would do a search on the internet for a horse hotel in that area. She came up with several, but there was one that jumped out at me. It was called "Hoof Prints," the same title as my book. I decided that's where we would stay. And so we left Carlsbad and headed out across the desolate west Texas highway. The day was Thursday, August 30. It was Jim's and my twentieth wedding anniversary.

The proprietor of Hoof Prints Ranch, David, was welcoming and very helpful. The accommodations for the horses were comfortable and they had room to move around and graze. The following morning when were getting ready to leave, like the veterinarian, David also refused to take any money.

We left Stephenville and arrived safely back at Proud Spirit in the early afternoon. Jim met us at the gate while our dogs swarmed around us. We had eleven now and they were sniffing furiously at all the new smells we carried home on the tires of the truck and trailer. I wondered what tales these strange scents were telling the pups.

Were they telling them of a woman in Austin who wouldn't let go of the right thing to do? Or of the friends of Proud Spirit, one of whom stepped up without question or hesitation and offered to transport two horses he had never met, or the other friend who dropped everything in her own life, threw a change of clothes in a bag, and helped make the arduous four-day drive? Did the mysterious odors tell the story of a reclusive park ranger who held onto a powerful love for his horses and the belief that they deserved to live? Was there anything there that hinted at the generosity of strangers, the ones who allowed two old horses to rest over night and then wouldn't accept payment? Could my dogs smell the desert sand from a tiny little town in west Texas and the gentle man who lived there? "A town is its people," he said. A country is its people as well and I had just experienced some of our best.

I go through life relentlessly holding onto the tenet that our time here on earth is not about ourselves. It is about what we can give to the world around us. How we can make things better. The gesture can be as small as planting a flower garden for your horticulturally challenged sister or as grand as Bill Gates donating billions to charity. We all have a capacity to give without expecting anything in return, but in our diversity as human beings not everyone can see the reciprocity of this concept, as evidenced by the seemingly endless phone calls and e-mails from people asking us to take in a horse they no longer wanted to care for. I had left on this trip amid feelings of decided weariness from it all. It had become exhausting. My salvation and restoration was in the good of everyone involved in saving the lives of these two horses. I would never forget this experience.

We unloaded Poco and Slick, the two boys from Guadalupe. They had fared well throughout the trip, but were anxious to get out of the trailer. Gary had kept both horses shod and I would have the shoes removed before turning them out with the herd. So we led them to a large paddock where I gave them some fresh hay and let them settle in. I looked up at Jim as we leaned against a fence and watched the two horses eat.

"Happy anniversary," I said.

"Yeah," he laughed. "You too." He paused for just a second. "I didn't get you anything," he added.

I looked over at the two new horses and smiled. "Yeah, you did."

The Horses of Proud Spirit by Melanie Sue Bowles. There are approximately seven million horses in the United States. Each year, over 70,000 end up going to slaughter. Hundreds of thousands more are abused, neglected, or abandoned by callous and irresponsible owners. With a heart as big as a pasture, author Melanie Bowles takes some of these horses into her sanctuary called Proud Spirit. Here, horses that arrive listless and broken find a home where they finally know safety.

The bond between horse and caretaker does not happen overnight. It hangs by a fine thread of trust, which the author earns with endless patience and a full commitment to the well-being of the horses in her care. The horses, some of which have suffered severe abuse, astound her time and again with their ability to trust, return the love they are given, and enjoy the companionship of other horses.

You will meet an entire stableful of remarkable horses:
- Dusty, a young Thoroughbred who recovered from severe injuries to reveal a rambunctious personality and a knack for stealing hats
- Maddy, an elderly mare, and Dancer, a gallant Appaloosa, both of whom had been isolated for years but whose ecstatic first acquaintance at Proud Spirit was, mysteriously, like the reunion of two soul mates
- Annie, a little sorrel mare who will break your heart with her weary kindness and who found peace, at last, under an old oak tree in a pasture at Proud Spirit
- Wrangler, a Miniature whose premature separation from his dam turned him into a tiny tormentor. His rowdy innocence helped Marshal, a huge palomino Draft horse with neurological trauma, become playful and engaged as he educated Wrangler in horsy manners.

The Horses of Proud Spirit is an homage to the spirit of these alluring creatures and a memoir of lessons learned in compassion, strength, and loss. (hb)

• • •

Florida Horse Owner's Field Guide, 2nd edition by Marty Marth. Accurate, easy-to-read guide to selecting, caring for, and enjoying a horse in Florida. The only horse book devoted to Florida's special challenges of heat, humidity, insects, poisonous plants, and unique varieties of hay. Many helpful tips and quotes from top horse people. Includes updated information about equestrian trails in state parks.

Just a few of the tips you'll find in this field guide: What should be in every horse medicine cabinet? What is often the first clue that your horse may be sick? Which breeds may have arrived with the Spanish conquistadors? Where should you report a stolen horse in Florida? How can you get that frightened or stubborn horse into a trailer? (pb)